Your Miniature Schnauzer

By Mildred L. Doud

Compiled and Edited by
William W. Denlinger and R. Annabel Rathman

DENLINGER'S

Fairfax, Virginia 22030

Foreword

"Juno" peeked from behind the door frame of the den in her home. My husband and I saw a little black nose, and finally the entire alert, be-whiskered, curious face of an eight-month-old puppy. This was our first personal introduction to the Miniature Schnauzer.

We had waited six months for this opportunity, for Miniature Schnauzers were still rather scarce in our area in the early sixties. By lucky chance alone on our part, the "Juno" we adopted that day was a Ch. Delfin Janus ex Ch. Delfin Victoria daughter from the kennels of Mrs. Mae Dickenson. Tragically, though, because of her untimely death, Juno was with us for only three weeks; but in that brief time she had fascinated and charmed us completely with her style, personality, and background. We had become committed to the breed and knew that we had to become more involved.

Two months later with the purchase of a wee puppy from the Top Notch dogs of Mr. and Mrs. John Hardie, and with more help from them than words can tell, this involvement opened and expanded into an engrossing hobby full of happy times and heartaches, too, for us. It has included association with some of the nicest people in the world —dog people—who so willingly have given of their time to teach and guide the newcomer about these little four-legged gems.

I have included much of this shared information in this book, and breeders and fanciers have been most generous in allowing the use of their pictures, records, and anecdotes.

M. L. D.

To Bob with my thanks.

Copyright © 1974.

By William W. Denlinger, Fairfax, Virginia 22030
All rights reserved, including the right to reproduce this book, or portions thereof, in any form, except for the inclusion of brief quotations in a review. This book was completely manufactured in the United States of America and published simultaneously in Canada by General Publishing Company, Toronto, Canada.

International Standard Book Number: 0-87714-015-4

Library of Congress Catalog Card Number: 73-84514

Contents

The Miniature Schnauzer Puppy   5
The Adult Miniature Schnauzer   13
Grooming for Show   21
Grooming and General Coat Care   33
Nutrition   39
Maintaining the Dog's Health   45
Housing Your Dog   53
History of the Genus *Canis*   57
History of the Miniature Schnauzer   65
The Breed in Other Countries   71
Personality of the Miniature Schnauzer   73
The Miniature Schnauzer in the Obedience Ring   77
Pillars of the Breed   85
Manners for the Family Dog   97
Bench Shows   105
Obedience Competition   111
Genetics   117
Breeding and Whelping   123
Winning Miniature Schnauzers   129
American Miniature Schnauzer Club Specialty, New York   131
American Miniature Schnauzer Club Specialty, Pennsylvania   136
Westminster Kennel Club Show   144
International Kennel Club Show   153

The Author, Mildred L. Doud, and Ch. Carrousel Lafitte.

The Miniature Schnauzer Puppy

He's small but sturdy and very stylish, and he doesn't shed or have a characteristic doggy odor. He is alert, friendly, intelligent, and a devoted companion. No wonder that interest in the Miniature Schnauzer has skyrocketed during the past few years!

How does one locate just THE right Miniature Schnauzer once the decision is made to purchase a member of this delightful breed? First, it would be wise for the prospective buyer to evaluate and determine his own needs honestly according to his living conditions, purposes in wanting a Miniature Schnauzer, finances, and personal preferences. For example, does he work all day? Does he live in the top floor of a high-rise apartment? Does he have very young children? Any of these circumstances might create difficulties both for a young puppy and for the owner, so that an older dog might better suit the situation. Does the buyer have preferences regarding color, size, or sex? Is he interested in showing or breeding, or is the addition intended to be totally a pet? By thinking about these factors, the prospective buyer can narrow his field of search and concentrate on the requirements he wishes to fill.

The best place to buy a Miniature Schnauzer is from a credible breeder. A credible breeder has a sincere interest in the care and the quality of his dogs. He tries to breed Miniature Schnauzers that come as close as possible in both conformation and temperament to the Standard of Perfection of the breed. He has the knowledge to answer questions about breed specifics and proper care. His premises are clean and orderly. He is just as concerned that his Miniature Schnauzer is going to the right home as the buyer is in obtaining just the right puppy for his needs. A reliable breeder will readily provide the buyer with a pedigree, registration papers, a complete health record, and information about the puppy's feeding, grooming, and general care. He will guarantee quality and health as represented at the time of the sale. The exchange of money does not end his interest in the puppy.

Breeders can be located by attending dog shows, by reading various dog publications, and by checking with kennel clubs. Also, a prospective purchaser may write to The American Kennel Club, Inc. (51 Madison Avenue, New York, New York 10010), and request a list of Miniature Schnauzer breeders in his area.

Show dogs and pet dogs come from the same litter, and they require identical early care. Selection of a pet dog may be made at an early age, but the selection of show or breeding stock should be postponed until as late an age as possible, for it is imperative that such animals possess certain specific structural qualities which to a great extent simply take time to develop. By six months of age a puppy usually can be compared to the official breed Standard much more reliably. While he still may change for better or for worse, and he still needs time to mature (up to two years of age in some instances), he can be evaluated more positively than can an eight-week-old puppy. The fact that an animal is purebred, registered, costs X amount of dollars, or comes from such and such stock, does not render him faultless! A Miniature Schnauzer that appears to be a show prospect at three months may not maintain this potential by eight months of age, or, though a rarity, the ugly duckling may blossom into a swan. Remember that a dog's pedigree is only as good as the dogs in it. The dog's genes coupled with his care and environment will determine his eventual appearance and behavior.

The majority of dogs sold are wanted solely as pets, and though they should remain pets, they are not "just" pets. They are beloved members of their families, and pet buyers deserve specimens that are the best looking and have the best disposition available. However, the pet buyer must not be disappointed if his dog is not constructed exactly like the show winners.

Health, condition, and soundness are primary and paramount factors to consider in the selection of a Miniature Schnauzer puppy. In general, the puppy should be clean, combed, and sweet-smelling. His eyes should be clear and bright; his coat should be glossy, his skin supple and free of scales and parasites; gums should be pink; and teeth should be white. A puppy should be roly-poly—neither too thin nor bloated. Check for umbilical hernia. Check a male's testicles (lack of one or both disqualifies a male from conformation showing and from breeding). Inquire about fecal checks for worms and appropriate inoculations against distemper, hepatitis, leptospirosis, and rabies. Nails should be short. With Miniature Schnauzers there are other specific requirements which should be checked: front and rear dewclaws should be removed, the tail should be docked properly, and the ears should be cropped and healing nicely (or healed). The reliable breeder usually has cropping done between seven and ten weeks of age.

Typical Miniature Schnauzer puppy temperament should be friendly, curious, and comfortably outgoing, but when puppy shop-

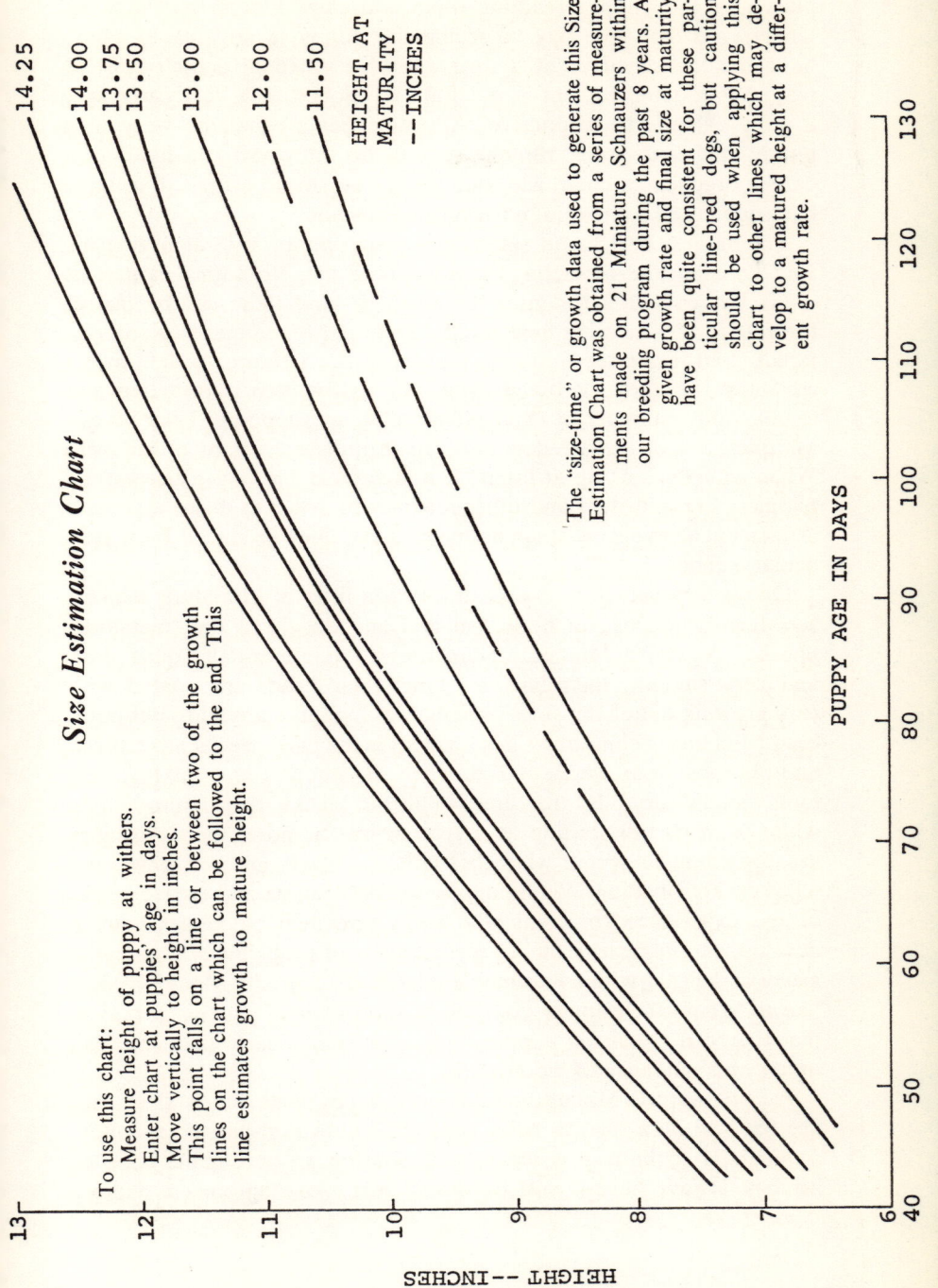

ping, give the puppy breathing room and allow him to set the pace. Understand that you may be seeing the puppy in an area to which he is unaccustomed or at a time when his schedule doesn't call for play. While temperament is not fully developed at a very early age, a puppy should be responsive. All things being equal, be wary of a puppy that consistently runs away with his tail down and hides in a corner or under a chair. He may always be shy to a fault. Excessive barking may be a cover for a nervous disposition.

The hardest part about selecting a young puppy is in analyzing his conformation and predicting the adult outcome. No animal is perfect —his virtues and faults must be weighed—and there can be no set formula for determining final results. Different bloodlines develop differently; structure needs time to mature. It is, therefore, to the buyer's advantage to study the breed avidly through written information and to talk with a number of fanciers before puppy shopping. Then he can ask questions of the breeders and can formulate opinions of his own. When actually looking at litters, it is helpful if the buyer can see the puppies' sire and dam and other relatives in order to make a general assessment of type and temperament of the dogs produced by a particular kennel.

One is fortunate if he is able to follow a litter of Miniature Schnauzers from whelping, for he will marvel and delight at the "metamorphosis." Newborn Miniature Schnauzer coats are usually quite dark and very smooth, their tails are long, their heads are domed with ears growing out of the sides—the babies look like anything but purebred Miniature Schnauzers! But changes in the early weeks are radical, and by about four weeks of age, when the puppies are walking, they look "Schnauzery." By that time, in all but blacks, that distinguishing white beard is just starting as a spot below the nose, the furnishings are beginning to sprout white beneath the black, and eyebrows and whiskers are bristling. When puppies are between six and twelve weeks of age, experienced breeders who know how their bloodlines tend to develop, can begin to estimate certain areas of problems and potential (such as height) with a reasonable degree of accuracy. Many breeders like to groom the puppies completely sometime during this period so that they can assess the puppies' anatomy more clearly than they can under an abundance of woolly hair.

An ungroomed Miniature Schnauzer puppy coat that is sleek and lies flat will be a quality adult coat. The cute fluff-ball of a puppy, particularly if the coat is wavy, may develop an acceptable coat, or he may always have a soft or mixed coat. An ungroomed puppy's body coat is not always a reliable indicator of his adult color, with the exception of puppies born white or parti-color. These will never change and represent breed disqualifications. Sometimes puppies thought to be black at birth may develop grizzle with time. In salt and peppers and black and silvers, look for good pigmentation in the face, for this coloring will remain and it adds a great deal to a Schnauzer's expression. Furnishings that are profuse and cottony at three months will be that way permanently, while puppy furnishings that are sparse may or may not develop adequately.

Look for a scissors bite, for overshot or undershot puppy occlusion will rarely correct itself; however, one cannot feel safe about bite until the second teeth are firmly established at five or six months of age. Study the head. A snipy muzzle will never fill out properly; large round and/or light eyes will never change for the better. Splayed feet, extreme cowhocks, low tail and ear set, and light bones will never correct themselves. Gait usually does not settle until about five months of age, so while gait cannot be appraised accurately in a youngster, tight elbows, well-arched paws, and good angulation should be evident.

Look for a squarely built, happy, robust puppy with a "twelve o'clock" tail. Formulate a mental picture of a typey and "balanced" puppy and look for a puppy that conforms as closely as possible to this mental image. ("Balance" means that all of the puppy's parts are in pleasing proportion in relation to each other, though puppies are known to grow in different directions at different stages.) When lifted, the puppy should feel well-bodied and dense—the "paperweight" type of puppy, I call him. Go over the puppy point for point according to the Standard, if you can. He cannot be evaluated numerically and rated "pass" or "fail" because the breed Standard presently has no point system. You cannot expect mature qualities in a puppy, but you can tally in a general way the attributes and weaknesses of the moment. Most weaknesses do not improve appreciably.

Most important of all, there should be a mutual appeal between the puppy and the prospective owner.

Don't take the newly selected puppy or grown dog home until you have made adequate preparations for him **PRIOR** to his arrival. His immediate needs for a draft-free, safe sleeping place, for proper exercise and nutrition, and for medical and emotional care should be considered and proper arrangements made. Rely on the breeder's suggestions in these matters to make the transition easier for all concerned. To bring a puppy into a household during what might be a very busy

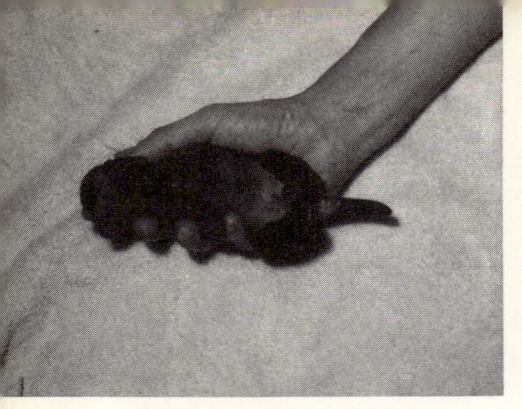 Half-day-old puppy. Eyes and ears sealed. Note white area on tail. Many use this as guide and dock tails at top of white spot.

 Salt and pepper puppy, 13 hours old.

or very sad time is not fair to the puppy or the members of the household. When the day for the adoption finally arrives, many owners find that morning, when everyone is fresh, is the best time for the trip. If possible, hold the puppy carefully on a towel on your lap during the ride—he will appreciate the feeling of security this will give him. If you are transporting the puppy by yourself and therefore must also do the driving, then, for everyone's safety, put the puppy in a box or a crate and place it where you and the puppy can see each other.

As a safeguard for both the buyer and the seller, it is advisable for the new owner to have the puppy examined by a veterinarian as soon as possible. I always suggest that the Miniature Schnauzer be held while in the veterinarian's waiting room, for I personally feel that this is not the place for animals to socialize. On this first visit take along the puppy's medical record to date for the veterinarian's information, and a fecal sample. Become informed as to the veterinarian's desired schedule for future required inoculations.

Litter of nine from Barclay Square.

With the exception of those cases where both parties sign a written agreement establishing the fact that registration papers will be omitted for one reason or another, the seller should provide the buyer with registration papers—either an application for individual registration or the actual A.K.C. certificate. In either case, the papers must be completed by both the seller and the buyer in accordance with the instructions on the form. The buyer then mails the form with the required fee to the A.K.C. and within several weeks, he, as new owner, will receive a certificate showing that the dog is registered in his name. It is imperative that the buyer send the registration papers to The American Kennel Club as soon as possible.

If the breeder has not already filed the individual registration papers, the buyer will receive the blue individual registration application, and he may select a name for the puppy. A first and second choice of names is required. Usually the breeder will wish to have his kennel name or prefix used, but it should not be used without his permission. The prefix is to be followed by a name, and the total number of letters of this combination may not exceed twenty-five. An original name should be chosen, for over-used names will not be accepted by the A.K.C. The dog's call name at home may be anything the owners choose—like or totally unlike the registered name. There are many "Whiskers" and "Saltys" romping at home, identified to the A.K.C. by more unusual or sophisticated titles! Once a puppy name has been accepted by the A.K.C. and the dog is given a registration number, neither may be changed even though ownership may be transferred any number of times.

Future champion from Rosehill Kennels.

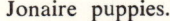

Jonaire puppies.

A Jonaire puppy.

Eng. Ch. Risepark Bon-Ell Taurus. Photo by Sally Anne Thompson, London, England.

Ch. Tiger Bo Von-Riptide, first black and silver champion since 1931.

The Adult Miniature Schnauzer

A dog is not officially considered an adult until he reaches twelve months of age, but, depending on his maturing rate, much of the following can be applied to a somewhat younger individual.

An overview of characteristics of an adult Miniature Schnauzer must be prefaced with the breed Standard, for it is only against this official Standard, which has been approved by The American Kennel Club, Inc., that the Miniature Schnauzer should be evaluated.

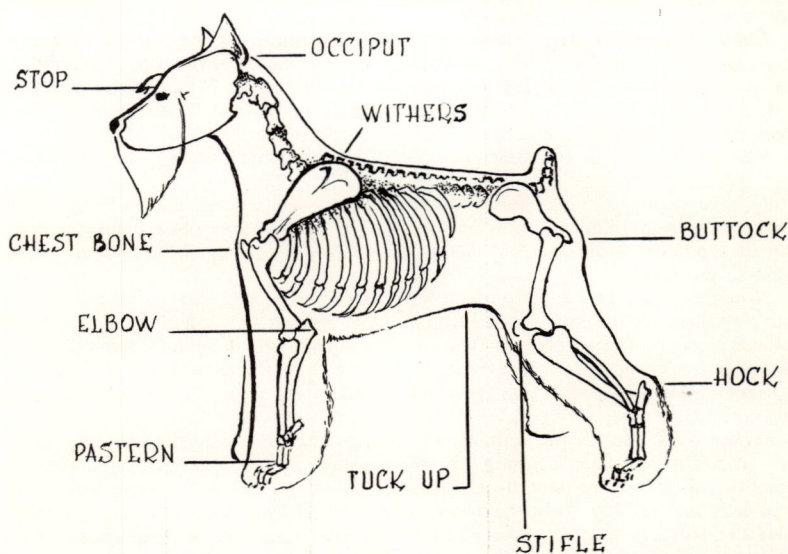

Height is measured from withers to ground. To measure, make certain dog is standing in naturally alert pose with forelegs vertical. Without official measuring device (Phillips Measuring Stand), one can attain reasonable measurement by using yardstick vertically, and placing spatula across withers (shoulder blades) perpendicular to yardstick.
Length is measured from chest bone to buttock.

STANDARD FOR THE MINIATURE SCHNAUZER

General Appearance—The Miniature Schnauzer is a robust, active dog of Terrier type, resembling his larger cousin, the Standard Schnauzer, in general appearance, and of an alert, active disposition. He is sturdily built, nearly square in proportion of body length to height, with plenty of bone, and without any suggestion of Toyishness.

Head—Strong and rectangular, its width diminishing slightly from ears to eyes, and again to the tip of the nose. The forehead is unwrinkled. The top skull is flat and fairly long. The foreface is parallel to the top skull, with a slight stop; and it is at least as long as the top skull. The muzzle is strong in proportion to the skull; it ends in a moderately blunt manner, with thick whiskers which accentuate the rectangular shape of the head.

Teeth—The teeth meet in a scissors bite. That is, the upper front teeth overlap the lower front teeth in such a manner that the inner surface of the upper incisors barely touches the outer surface of the lower incisors when the mouth is closed.

Eyes—Small, dark brown and deep-set. They are oval in appearance and keen in expression.

Ears—When cropped the ears are identical in shape and length, with pointed tips. They are in balance with the head and not exaggerated in length. They are set high on the skull and carried perpendicularly at the inner edges, with as little bell as possible along the outer edges. When uncropped the ears are small and V-shaped, folding close to the skull.

Neck—Strong and well arched, blending into the shoulders, and with the skin fitting tightly at the throat.

Body—Short and deep, with the brisket extending at least to the elbows. Ribs are well sprung and deep, extending well back to a short loin. The underbody does not present a tucked-up appearance at the flank. The topline is straight; it declines slightly from the withers to the base of the tail. The over-all length from chest to stern bone equals the height at the withers.

Forequarters—The forequarters have flat, somewhat sloping shoulders and high withers. Forelegs are straight and parallel when viewed from all sides. They have strong pasterns and good bone. They are separated by a fairly deep brisket which precludes a pinched front. The elbows are close, and the ribs spread gradually from the first rib so as to allow space for the elbow to move close to the body.

Hindquarters—The hindquarters have strong-muscled, slanting thighs; they are well bent at the stifles and straight from hock to so-called heel. There is sufficient angulation so that, in stance, the hocks extend beyond the tail. The hindquarters never appear overbuilt or higher than the shoulders.

Feet—Short and round (cat-feet) with thick, black pads. The toes are arched and compact.

Action—The trot is the gait at which movement is judged. The dog must gait in a straight line. Coming on, the forelegs are parallel, with the elbows close to the body. The feet turn neither inward nor outward. Going away, the hind legs are parallel from the hocks down, and travel wide. Viewed from the side, the forelegs have a good reach, while the hind legs have a strong drive with good pick-up of hocks.

Tail—Set high and carried erect. It is docked only long enough to be clearly visible over the topline of the body when the dog is in proper length of coat.

Coat—Double, with a hard, wiry outer coat and a close undercoat. The body coat should be plucked. When in show condition, the proper length is not less than three-quarters of an inch except on neck, ears and skull. Furnishings are fairly thick but not silky.

Size—From 12 to 14 inches. Ideal size 13½ inches. *See disqualifications.*

Color—The recognized colors are salt and pepper, black and silver, and solid black. The typical color is salt and pepper in shades of gray; tan shading is permissible. The salt and pepper mixture fades out to light gray or silver white in the eyebrows, whiskers, cheeks, under throat, across chest, under tail, leg furnishings, under body, and inside legs. The light under-body hair is not to rise higher on the sides of the body than the front elbows.

The black and silvers follow the same pattern as the salt and peppers. The entire salt and pepper section must be black.

Black is the only solid color allowed. It must be a true black with no gray hairs and no brown tinge except where the whiskers may have become discolored. A small white spot on the chest is permitted.

Faults

Type—Toyishness, raciness, or coarseness.
Structure—Head coarse and cheeky. Chest too broad or shallow in brisket. Tail set low. Sway or roach back. Bowed or cowhocked hindquarters. Loose elbows.
Action—Sidegaiting. Paddling in front, or high hackney knee action. Weak hind action.
Coat—Too soft or too smooth and slick in appearance.
Temperament—Shyness or viciousness.
Bite—Undershot or overshot jaw. Level bite.
Eyes—Light and/or large and prominent in appearance.

Disqualifications

Dogs or bitches under 12 inches or over 14 inches.
Color solid white or white patches on the body.

SOME DEVIATIONS FROM THE IDEAL

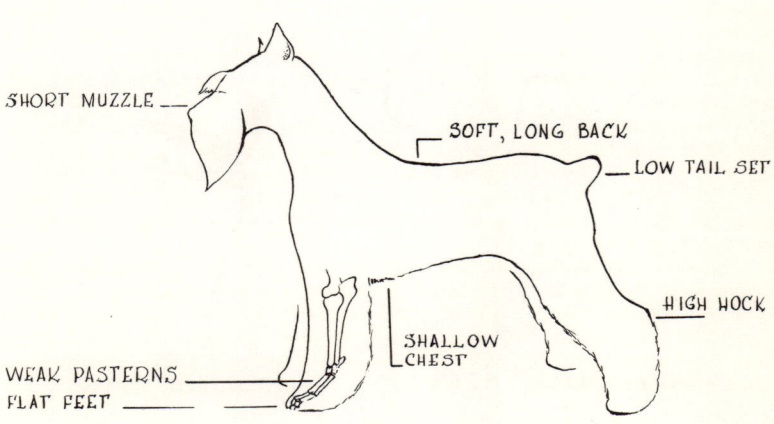

This Miniature Schnauzer Breed Standard was formulated by the American Miniature Schnauzer Club (the last revision was in 1958) and subsequently approved by The American Kennel Club to define the ideal Miniature Schnauzer. It also outlines faults and breed disqualifications; however, interpretation of the Standard is somewhat of an individual matter. Opinions regarding the severity of each fault vary, and individual preferences and evaluations weigh the dog's parts and interpret the written terms differently. It is for these reasons that some variations in "type" of Miniature Schnauzer occur, all fitting well within the Standard and winning in the conformation ring. Today we hear reference to the Terrier type, and to the Schnauzer type, the latter being a stockier, broader animal (though by no means coarse) than the more streamlined Terrier type with its straighter shoulders and elongated head. Changes in type or style may emerge over passing decades. Thus, we now also hear the description of an "old-fashioned" Schnauzer, referring to that type possessing very harsh coat and furnishings and one with perhaps fewer furnishings and less contrasting coloration, reminiscent of early Schnauzers.

To aid in interpretation of the official written word, the American Miniature Schnauzer Club has prepared an excellent booklet with a self-explanatory title, *The Illustrated Discussion of the Miniature Schnauzer Standard*. I commend this specialized publication to anyone who is interested in studying the breed, or in breeding or showing a Miniature Schnauzer.

HEAVY, SHORT NECK   UNDERSHOT BITE

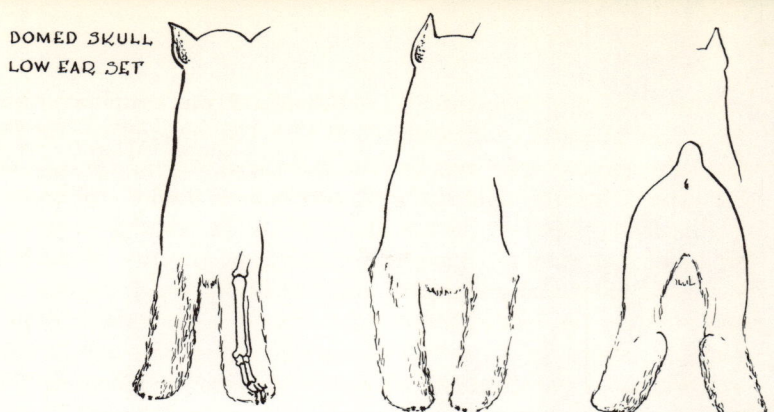

PINCHED FRONT — TOEING OUT.   LOOSE ELBOWS AND   COWHOCKED
                                TOEING IN.

No Miniature Schnauzer is anatomically perfect, and like the tides, areas of concern and improvement change over the years. Hard as the dedicated breeder strives to produce the epitome, every dog has faults. It is the degree of and number of faults weighed against a dog's virtues which determine his quality and categorize him pet or potential prize winner. In analyzing a dog, look at him as a whole being—including his personality—and not at each fault or virtue as the end in itself. Yet, do not discount the fact that a dog is a composite of parts, which, in the case of a purebred, should adhere as closely as possible to the desirable features set forth in the breed Standard. Look for a balanced silhouette in the adult Miniature Schnauzer, with height and length about equal.

While it is not the intent here to initiate complete discussions of "parts," I will make mention of the head, as any head unit is always considered one major distinguishing portion of any breed. A good Miniature Schnauzer head always reminds me of a shoe box—lean, strong, and rectangular, with good length of muzzle with good fill. Any

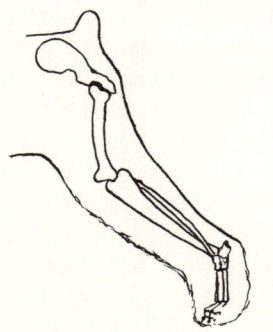   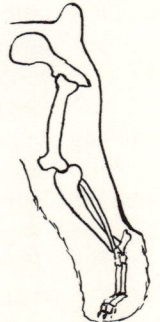

OVER — ANGULATION   STRAIGHT STIFLES
                           LACK OF ANGULATION

Ch. Sky Rocket's Uproar. Amateur handled by Mrs. Frank Ferguson, he set record during 1971 for most dogs ever defeated in breed competition. (Photo by William P. Gilbert.)

bite other than a scissors bite is a fault. Cropped ears should be set high and carried erect. Small dark eyes, correct carriage of the head, and deep facial pigmentation complete the typical expression.

It is helpful if one can attend as many dog shows as possible to see Miniature Schnauzers in action and to compare the living being to the Standard. Dogs with breed disqualifications cannot be shown in conformation classes, and, in addition to these, the A.K.C. rules disqualify dogs which are blind, castrated, spayed, have had their appearance changed by artificial means (except as specified in the Standard), or males exhibiting orchidism. However, these dogs can be enjoyed as fine pets and obedience workers.

Notice the variances in color and texture of the stripped coats, another feature which sets the Miniature Schnauzer apart from other breeds. The three recognized colors are solid black, black and silver, and salt and pepper, the latter being the most popular of the three and the one with a wide range of acceptable shading. However, a pale, washed-out looking salt and pepper is undesirable and will not change.

Among other observable features, gait has established itself by adulthood and represents a combination of bone structure and muscular development. It is a real delight to watch a properly constructed specimen move "like a train," as some will describe the correct parallel action with good reach in the front and great drive in the rear. Faulty movement (travelling too narrow, rope walking, out at the elbows, toeing in or out, stilted action, etc.) has concerned breeders for many years. To a degree, weak movement (and sagging toplines) can be improved with daily road work when the problem results from lack of muscular development. Road work involves walking the dog with his head up, at a good pace on a hard surface for a minimum of a mile a day. However, bone structure cannot be changed.

Though there are exceptions to everything, I like to consider adult height attained by about eight months of age. However, final maturity (settling-in and filling-out) may take up to two years. The allowable size range is twelve to fourteen inches at the highest point of the shoulders (the withers), with the ideal size currently set at thirteen and a half inches. Many people feel that large size is becoming a problem area, with too many Miniature Schnauzers either pushing the limit or going over. On the other hand, Miniature Schnauzers are not Toy dogs and should never appear that way. Even the adult twelve-incher with correct heavy bone and good rib spring will appear sturdily built and "Schnauzery."

Other characteristics to look for or to avoid in the adult Miniature Schnauzer are identical to those to be sought or to be avoided in puppyhood. Such features can be analyzed with no guesswork by adulthood, for temperament and conformation are established unquestionably in a mature, healthy dog.

Clever grooming techniques can improve the appearance of any dog as much as poor grooming will destroy the overall picture of a Miniature Schnauzer. Correct grooming, this frosting on the cake, is half the joy (and frustration) of "Schnauzerdom," but it cannot totally compensate for a lack of well-being or the proper structure underneath.

Ch. Johnson's Ebony Kwicksilver, first American-bred black Miniature Schnauzer bitch to finish in this country in over thirty years.

1959 photographs of Best-in-Show winner Ch. Yankee Pride Colonel Stump.

Note balance, topline, head, front, and rear.

Grooming for Show

In order to have a non-shedding canine, the owner must assume responsibility for his dog's periodic grooming. Don't own a Miniature Schnauzer unless you are willing to keep him looking like one!

Normal maintenance grooming of a Miniature Schnauzer is uncomplicated. As with any breed, the Miniature Schnauzer should be allotted time routinely for clipping or filing of the nails (ideally, the nails should be kept short—at one-quarter inch), for cleaning excretions from the inner corner of the eyes with damp cotton, if necessary, and for checking the skin, mouth, and so on for any irregularities. For all grooming work, the Miniature Schnauzer should be trained from puppyhood to stand on a sturdy table. Grooming time should be pleasant, but remember that you are the boss. Puppies that wiggle and nip may be considered cute and playful, but puppies grow up to be dogs, and since a Miniature Schnauzer is going to require grooming the rest of his life, he must understand what is expected of him. Be gentle but firm.

Specifically, the Miniature Schnauzer must be combed thoroughly with a metal comb with particular attention being paid to all the furnishings and whiskers so that mats will not develop. Should a mat form, try to work it out with your fingers, or split it in several places in the direction of hair growth with scissors, and then gently comb it out. If this fails, the mats will simply have to be cut out.

Leg furnishings should first be combed upward, making sure that the comb's teeth go all the way down to the dog's skin; then they should be combed downward, leaving the legs looking full. If necessary, legs furnishings and whiskers should be washed, dried, and thoroughly combed again. The hair on the bottom of the pads should be scissored even with the pads; hair on the vulva, penis, and anus should be kept scissored short for purposes of cleanliness. The ear canal should be kept free of hair by pulling it out with tweezers or the fingers. Once a week is usually adequate for these measures, and this regular care will keep general problem areas under control. However, the time will inevitably come when, because of length of hair, you're not sure your dog is still a Miniature Schnauzer and only a complete grooming will restore his identity.

Complete grooming of the Miniature Schnauzer is partly manual labor and partly an art. If one wishes to learn how to groom, it is suggested that he learn both from seeing and by doing. Study pictures and study dogs at the shows, and, if possible, watch a professional groom a Miniature Schnauzer. Check with local kennel clubs, for many Miniature Schnauzer groups periodically offer grooming instruction sessions. Formulate a mental picture of the finished product desired, and then settle down to the task and do it. Proficiency will come only with practice.

The Miniature Schnauzer is a double coated dog. The outer coat, called the hard coat, is wiry; the undercoat, or soft coat, is usually fuzzy. The salt and pepper speckling of the hard coat is the result of banded hairs. This "agouti" pattern means that each individual hard hair is striped around with different measures of black and white, and/or rust. The amount and placement of the black in each hair determines whether the salt and pepper dog appears dark, light, or in-between. The hard coat of a black or black and silver is solid black.

If the Miniature Schnauzer is to possess the distinguishing hard body coat, he must be stripped or plucked. This means that the body hair must be pulled out at the roots—not cut. This is the only way that a hard coat can be retained, and this hard coat is a must if the dog is to be shown in breed competition.

The color of a salt and pepper's undercoat may be any variable of gray or tan, but this is no indication of the color of the hard coat. Blacks and black and silvers have black undercoats. The same basic method of grooming is used for all three colorations, and for puppies or adults. The puppy coat, however, is like no other coat that the Miniature Schnauzer will ever have again. Regardless of that fact, it can be handled in the same manner as an adult coat.

If the puppy coat is long enough to permit grooming, I like to do

a first stripping at six to seven weeks of age. This allows better evaluation of puppy conformation. This first stripping would be to remove the soft, black puppy hair.

An adult Miniature Schnauzer's hard coat is "blown," that is, the hair is dead and can be pulled out or stripped readily, when it is at least two inches long, but any stripping should be postponed if the dog is sick or if his skin is not in good condition. Remember, too, that this artificial removal of a dog's coat also removes his insulation and protection from the elements. Therefore, a sweater or coat is recommended to compensate for the loss of coat in the cold weather, and in the summer, the dog will need to be protected from sunburn and insects.

Basic tools needed for grooming are:

- Sturdy, slip-proof table. In addition, a grooming sling or comparable contrivance is a handy "extra hand."
- Stripping knives, sizes Medium and Fine. I suggest the use of stripping knives for stripping because I feel they make the job progress faster and more easily. However, if one prefers hand stripping, the fingers do the job. Do NOT use any kind of grooming tool with a razor blade in it.
- Comb, metal, size Medium. (The size refers to the spacing of the teeth.)
- Toenail clippers or file.
- Scissors. 1 barber type and 1 thinning shears.
- Helpful items are electric or hand clippers, mat splitter, grooming mitt, blood coagulant for the nails, tweezers, and white grooming chalk.

As one continues his grooming experiences, he will probably add many of the grooming aids which are available and which suit his preferences.

The grooming procedures described briefly here represent *fundamental* methods found to meet *basic* requirements for show or home. There are a number of correct variations practiced by expert groomers, but to enumerate all the fine points and techniques would require an entire book in itself! When the novice becomes confident and competent in basic technique, he can gear his knowledge to "custom groom" each individual on the basis of the dog's coat texture, conformation, and personality, to accentuate the dog's best features, and to try to camouflage the less-than-perfect areas. He may wish to experiment with rolling or rotating a coat, hand stripping, raking, and/or different clipping lengths.

Shaggy Ch. Carrousel Lafitte readying for stripping.

Top Notch Adagio Dancer and Ch. Carrousel Clarabo, demonstrating difference in appearance of clipped and stripped coats.

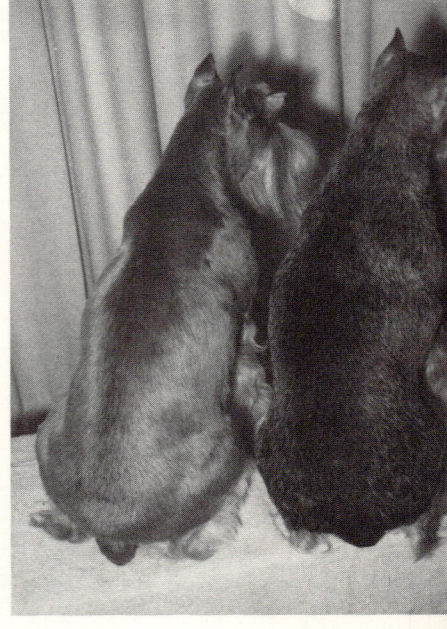

Beginning stripping. Note position of hands and stripping knife. Note difference in appearance of hard coat and soft coat.

ENTIRE BODY STRIPPING METHOD: (Removing hard coat of adult, and/or black, soft puppy hair.) See Chart I.

Two hands are needed for the stripping process—this is the manual labor part! The left hand grips the dog's skin to hold it taut while the right hand pulls the hair out with the stripping knife (or the thumb and forefinger if hand stripping is done). I like to start stripping at the dog's withers and work back, completely stripping sides, hind legs, and tail. I move to the occiput and complete all stripping of the neck and shoulders. Last I do the head, ears, and forechest. Holding the knife perpendicular to the dog's skin (this position is extremely important so as not to cut the coat), grasp small amounts of hard coat hair between the knife and thumb, close to the skin, and pull out the hair in the direction it grows. Use an arm and shoulder motion, and keep the wrist stiff. Concentrate stripping in a small area until all the hard coat has been removed there. The soft, short undercoat will remain. Then move on. Make sure that the coat is pulled out, not cut. If the coat has been pulled out correctly, the remaining undercoat will look uneven and feel soft. A cut coat will be more even, and it will feel bristly. Be sure to strip down to the elbows, down to the elbow line on the ribs, and strip in a curve to one inch above the hocks on the hind legs.

When stripping of all the hard coat has been completed, the groomer is ready for trimming; this is the effort and the art that give the Miniature Schnauzer his style and character. To trim effectively, one must develop an "eye" for and keep in mind an overall silhouette of the balanced image he wishes to create. I like to start trimming on the dog's abdomen with his right side facing me, and work my way around him. Trimming is done with scissors or clippers. See Chart II with its suggested list of steps for trimming procedure.

When all the trimming is finished, shorten the nails. (See page 38.)

Normally, a Miniature Schnauzer does not have that characteristic doggie odor, so it is not necessary—nor is it healthful—to give him a complete bath frequently; however, if a full body bath is desired, this is the time to do it, once the dog is six months old. Protect him from becoming chilled until he is thoroughly dry. After he is dry, he will require a thorough combing. (For instructions on bathing the dog, see page 36.)

Within five to seven weeks after the dog has been stripped, a new hard coat will sprout beneath the remaining soft coat. When you brush your hand from the dog's tail toward his head, you will feel the bristly new points breaking through the skin. The soft coat then

Chart I

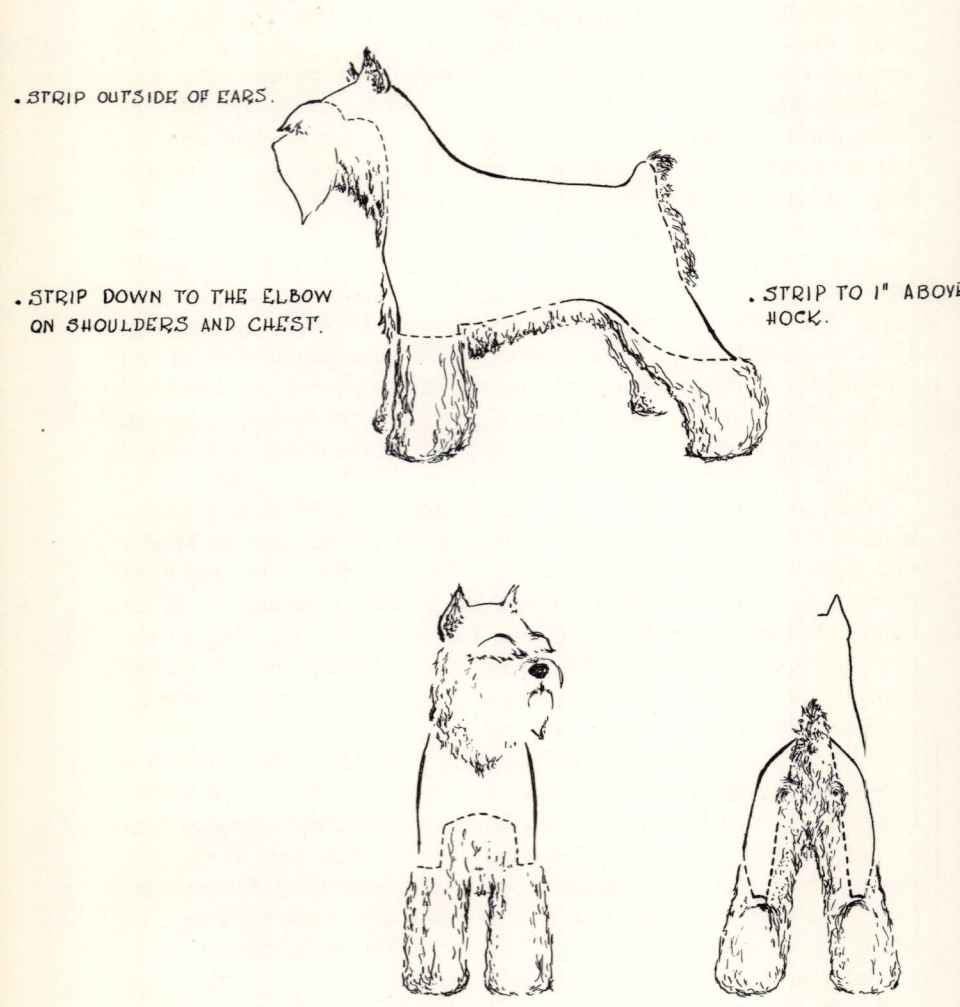

can be stripped out easily without damaging the new growth. One dare not wait longer than seven to eight weeks for this second stripping, or the hard coat will grow so long that it is difficult, if not impossible, to separate the two. For removal of the soft coat, the same stripping method is repeated; however, the finished dog will be wearing his new hard coat instead of his underwear. Trimming is identical. Blending of the "fringe" areas (where hard coat and clipped areas meet) may be done cautiously with thinning shears, if necessary. (Use the same system for the second puppy stripping.)

This two part system (stripping first the hard coat and then the soft coat) is usually done twice a year with trims in-between to keep areas of fast growth (ears, tummy, fanny, etc.) in check.

Basic Trimming Suggestions:
1. Clip abdomen close.
2. Taper chest hair to abdomen, being careful not to give a picture with too much tuck-up.
3. Comb furnishings out from leg and cut downward.
4. Comb furnishings forward and cut.
5. Clip rear close.
6. Comb furnishings toward the rear and cut. Trim close at the elbow and taper out. Excessively long furnishings frequently look stringy (especially those tending to be sparse) and unattractive. The final result of trimmed furnishings should be one of balance with the rest of the dog.
7. Comb furnishings and cut downward.
8. Repeat trimming of abdomen, chest hair, and quarters on the other side of the dog.
9. Clip cheeks and throat close. A good guide as to how much beard to leave is this: clip a line ¼ inch from outer corner of eye to about ½ inch forward from "mole" or "bump" on cheek, practically to corner of mouth, and to "bump" under chin.
10. Taper and trim.
11. Scissor hair inside of ears and pull hair from ear canals. Scissor hair on edges of ears.
12. Comb furnishings out to sides and trim.
13. Trim hair all around front feet to resemble cat's paw.
14. Comb hair to sides and cut. Repeat Step 13 on rear paws.
15. Lift each foot and scissor hair on bottom even with pads.
16. Cut nails.
17. Carefully blend "fringe" areas (where clipped and stripped areas meet) as necessary.

Chart II

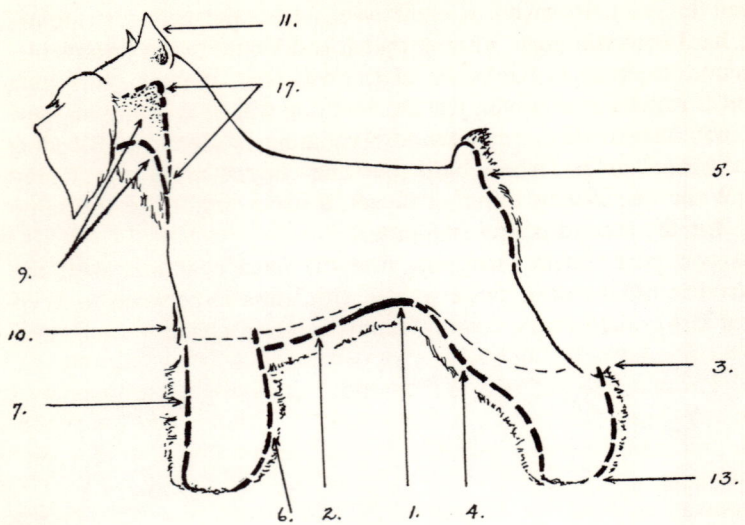

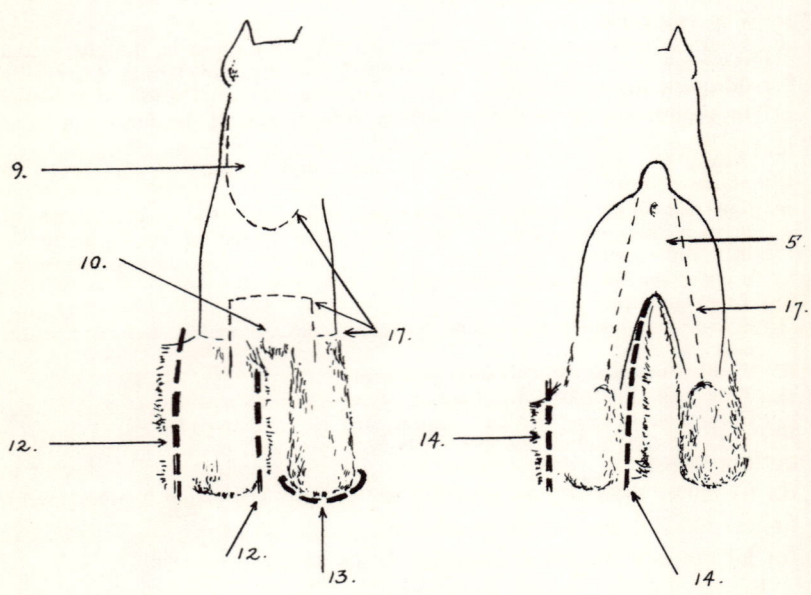

Basic Trimming

SECTIONAL STRIPPING (Chart III) is a method almost compulsory for dogs which are to be shown, and is desirable for anyone doing his own grooming. The stripping and trimming techniques are the same, but, because the head, neck, and fringe areas of the Miniature Schnauzer's coat always grow faster and fuller than the back areas, with this method the faster growing areas are stripped out later than the back in order to compensate for the difference in growth rates. While the Schnauzer will look rather like a lion or a clown with a ruff during part of the process, he will stay looking neat for a longer period of time when the hard coat finally is in full bloom. Three to four sections is a usual breakdown, but any system of pattern may be developed to sculpture a coat. Chart III shows a typical three-part sectional breakdown ("A" being stripped first, "B" second, and "C" third). The only precaution is that the time lapse between sections must not be any longer than ten days or a definite length and color variation will be apparent and this variation cannot be blended until the coat is rather long.

Preparing a Miniature Schnauzer for the breed ring and keeping him in condition for it is one of the most difficult, frustrating, and rewarding aspects of Miniature Schnauzer involvement. If a Miniature Schnauzer is to be shown, the hard coat on the back (section "A") must be removed about ten weeks prior to the first show. Different types of coats will develop at different rates, so the timing might vary for different individuals, but the coat on the back must be a minimum of three-quarters of an inch long for breed competition. A very hard textured coat can be worked better and will lie flatter longer than the softer, mixed, or wavy coat, but at best one has only about eight to nine weeks of showing time before the coat will look too shaggy for the breed ring.

A few days before each show, the dog will require trimming (but not too short and severe). Ears will need to be cleaned and the hair on the edges trimmed to give the ears a sharp outline, nails and feet must be trimmed, and fringe areas will need some consideration if the dog is to appear well groomed and stylish. All trimming and blending with the scissors must be done with great caution, for too zealous cutting will destroy the harsh texture of the hard coat. It is better to do as much blending as possible by pulling out straggling hair with fingers or stripping knife rather than to blend by cutting it. This is true for all three of the color varieties.

Before a show, the salt and pepper and black and silver dogs' white furnishings and whiskers must be washed. A little bluing added to

Chart III

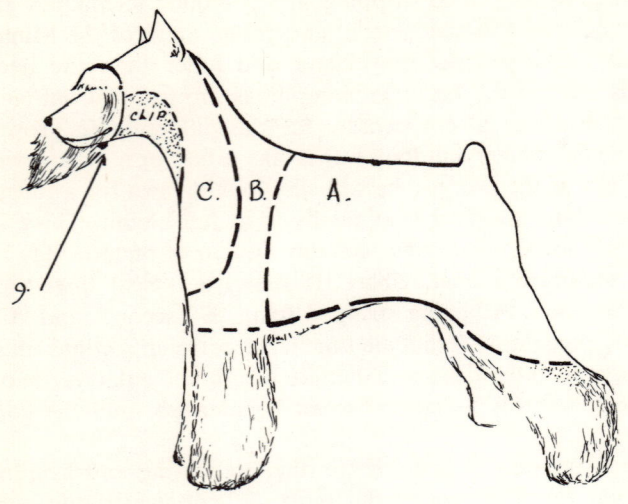

Strip between eyes as far down toward nose as about inner corner of eyes. Then trim any excess hair in an inverted "V" at top and "V" at bottom. Do not cut any hair under eyes.

Length of hair and eyebrow left at outer corner of eyes should balance with width of skull. Leave about ¼ inch.

Length of eyebrow must fit length of head. Comb eyebrow forward, and looking down on it, cut the desired length and then back at an angle to ¼ inch from outer corner of eye.

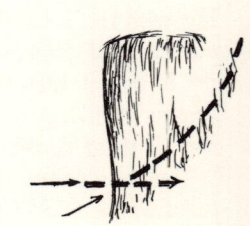

the rinse water will make them extra sparkly! At the show, soft white grooming chalk can be rubbed into all the white areas and then combed out thoroughly. This is a cleaning agent which makes the furnishings appear whiter and fuller. Dampen the furnishings, eyebrows, and whiskers with a little water or apply a little vanishing cream first so that the chalk will stick better. A bit of hair spray, carefully sprayed to avoid irritating the dog's eyes and genitals, will help keep the furnishings and brows in place, but the application of any other substances to change the color or quality of a coat violates A.K.C. rules.

A dog that is being prepared for the breed ring must be given special consideration if his furnishings and beard are to develop to their best advantage. Harsh furnishings grow slowly and break easily, so the dog possessing them cannot be allowed to race through tall grass, chew bones, play with other dogs, or engage in similar activities which would encourage breakage during his showing days. A daily light application of baby oil curbs breakage somewhat. Urine, saliva, eye secretions, food, mud, grass, and dirt may stain whiskers and furnishings, so attention to cleanliness is especially important. It is important to watch for possible skin eruptions, irritation, and external parasites, and to eradicate them should they occur.

Clipping: If a dog is solely a pet, or is to be shown only in obedience trials, or if the dog is ultra-sensitive to stripping because of age, skin condition, or personality, the owner may find it more practical to have him clipped entirely with electric or hand clippers. The Miniature Schnauzer pattern is identical for both stripping and clipping, so there is no excuse for poor pattern results. While clipping renders the salt and pepper dogs' coats gray, and all Schnauzers' coats soft and kitteny (in contradiction to the Standard), clipping has its advantages. It can be done any time that the owner desires (most choose about a three-month span, though some prefer a complete grooming every six weeks). Thus, the dog can be kept looking well groomed more consistently than the average owner is able or willing to do by stripping the coat. Also, the owner can choose any length of hair he wants and never has to have either a shaggy or a naked dog. Many owners prefer about a one-quarter-inch length of hair left on the back at clipping time, with the neck and head coats shorter. A dog which has been clipped can at a later time be groomed by stripping, but several strippings will be required to restore the original hard coat texture.

Remember that all outer beauty—the beautiful coat, the bright eyes, and the alert demeanor—starts with inner well-being.

Ch. Orbit's Agena-B (photo by Missy—1968). BOS, 1968 International Kennel Club Show. Whelped October 1965. A fourth generation champion of ORBIT, owned by Frances Cazier, Sepulveda, California.

Grooming and General Coat Care

Although coat types, textures, and patterns may seem purely arbitrary matters of little consequence, they are among the important characteristics that distinguish one breed from another. Actually, each breed has been developed to serve a specific purpose, and the coat that is considered typical for the breed is also the one most appropriate for the dog's specialized use—be it as guard, hunting companion, herder, or pet. A knowledge of the breed Standard approved by The American Kennel Club is helpful to the owner who takes pride in owning a well-groomed dog, typical of its breed.

Dogs with short, smooth coats (such as the Weimaraner, Basset, Beagle, smooth Dachshund and Chihuahua) usually shed only moderately and their coats require little routine grooming other than thorough brushing with a bristle brush or hound glove. For exhibition in the show ring, the whiskers, or "feelers," are trimmed close to the muzzle, but no other trimming is needed.

The wire coat of the Airedale, Wire Fox Terrier, Miniature Schnauzer, or Wirehaired Dachshund should be stripped or plucked in show trim at regular intervals. The dog can then be kept well groomed by thorough combing and brushing.

Curly coated breeds such as the Curly Coated Retriever, and the American and Irish Water Spaniels, generally require no special coat care other than frequent brushing. True curly coated breeds are very curly indeed and are not to be confused with breeds such as the Golden Retriever, Gordon Setter, Brittany Spaniel, and English Springer Spaniel, which have slightly curled or wavy coats of somewhat silky texture. The longer hair, or "feathers," typically found on tail, legs, ears, and chest of these breeds should be trimmed slightly to make the outline neater.

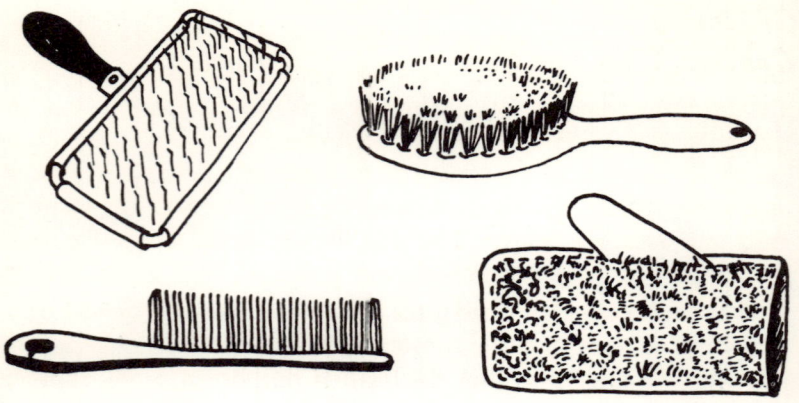

(UPPER LEFT) Wire brush (RIGHT) Bristle brush
(LOWER LEFT) Comb—Hound glove.

They are not "trimmed to pattern," however, as are such longhaired breeds as the Kerry Blue Terrier and the Poodle, which, when shown in the breed ring, must be clipped and trimmed in the patterns specified in the breed Standards.

The Longhaired Dachshund, the Borzoi, and the Yorkshire Terrier have long but comparatively silky coats, whereas the Newfoundland and the Rough Collie have long straight coats with rather harsh texture. Long coats must be kept brushed out thoroughly to eliminate mats and snarls.

The dog should be taught from puppyhood that a grooming session is a time for business, not for play. He should be handled gently, though, for it is essential to avoid hurting him in any way. Grooming time should be pleasant for both dog and master.

Tools required vary with the breed, but always include combs, brushes, and nail clippers and files. Combs should have wide-spaced teeth with rounded ends so that the dog's skin will not be scratched accidentally. For the same reason, brushes with natural bristles are usually preferable to those with synthetic bristles that may be too fine and sharp.

A light, airy, pleasant place in which to work is desirable, and it is of the utmost importance that neither dog nor master be distracted by other dogs, cats, or people. Consequently, it is usually preferable that grooming be done indoors.

Particularly for large or medium breeds, a sturdy grooming table is desirable. Many owners hold small puppies or Toy dogs during grooming sessions, athough it is better if they, too, are groomed on a table. Large and medium size dogs should be taught to jump onto the table and to jump off again when grooming is completed. Small dogs must be lifted on and off to avoid falls and possible injury. The dog should stand while the back and upper portions of the body are groomed, and lie on his side while underparts of his body are brushed, nails clipped, etc.

Before each session, the dog should be permitted to relieve himself. Once grooming is begun, it is important to avoid keeping the dog standing so long that he becomes tired. If a good deal of grooming is needed, it should be done in two or more short periods.

It is almost impossible to brush too much, and show dogs are often brushed for a full half hour a day, year round. If you cannot brush your dog every day, you should brush him a minimum of two or three times a week. Brushing removes loose skin particles and stimulates circulation, thereby improving condition of the skin. It also stimulates secretion of the natural skin oils that make the coat look healthy and beautiful.

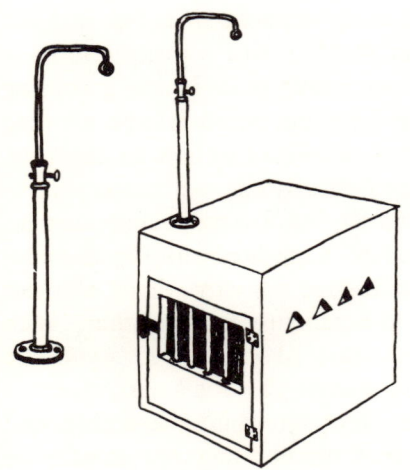

Dog crate with grooming—table top is ideal—providing rigid, well supported surface on which to groom dog, and serving as indoor kennel for puppy or grown dog. Rubber matting provides non-slip surface. Dog's collar may be attached to adjustable arm. Lightweight and readily transported yet sturdy, the crate is especially useful to owner who takes dog with him when he travels.

Before brushing, any burs adhering to the coat, as well as matted hair, should be carefully removed, using the fingers and coarse toothed comb with a gentle, teasing motion to avoid tearing the coat. The coat should first be brushed lightly in the direction in which the hair grows. Next, it should be brushed vigorously in the opposite direction, a small portion at a time, making sure the bristles penetrate the hair to the skin, until the entire coat has been brushed thoroughly and all loose soil removed. Then the coat should be brushed in the direction the hair grows, until every hair is sleekly in place.

The dog that is kept well brushed needs bathing only rarely. Once or twice a year is usually enough. Except for unusual circumstances when his coat becomes excessively soiled, no puppy under six months of age should be bathed in water. If it is necessary to bathe a puppy, extreme care must be exercised so that he will not become chilled. No dog should be bathed during cold weather and then permitted to go outside immediately. Whatever the weather, the dog should always be given a good run outdoors and permitted to relieve himself before he is bathed.

Various types of "dry baths" are available at pet supply stores. In general, they are quite satisfactory when circumstances are such that a bath in water is impractical. Dry shampoos are usually rubbed into the dog's coat thoroughly, then removed by vigorous towelling or brushing.

Before starting a water bath, the necessary equipment should be assembled. This includes a tub of appropriate size, and another tub or pail for rinse water. (A small hose with a spray nozzle—one that may be attached to the water faucet—is ideal for rinsing the dog.) A metal or plastic cup for dipping water, special dog shampoo, a small bottle of mineral or olive oil, and a supply of absorbent cotton should be placed nearby, as well as a supply of heavy towels, a wash cloth, and the dog's combs and brushes.

The amount of water required will vary according to the size of the dog, but should reach no higher than the dog's elbows. Bath water and rinse water should be slightly warmer than lukewarm, but should not be hot.

To avoid accidentally getting water in the dog's ears, place a small amount of absorbent cotton in each. With the dog standing in the tub, wet his body by using the cup to pour water over him. Take care to avoid wetting the head, and be careful to avoid getting water or shampoo in the eyes. (If you should accidentally do so, placing a few drops of mineral or olive oil in the inner corner of the eye will bring relief.) When the dog is thoroughly wet, put a small amount of shampoo on his back and work up a lather, rubbing briskly. Wash his entire body and then rinse as much of the shampoo as possible from the coat by dipping water from the tub and pouring it over the dog.

Dip the wash cloth into clean water, wring it out enough so it won't drip, then wash the dog's head, taking care to avoid the eyes. Remove the cotton from the dog's ears and sponge them gently, inside and out. Shampoo should never be used inside the ears, so if they are extremely soiled, sponge them clean with cotton saturated with mineral or olive oil. (Between baths, the ears should be cleaned frequently in the same way.)

Replace the cotton in the ears, then use the cup and container of rinse water (or hose and spray nozzle) to rinse the dog thoroughly. Quickly wrap a towel around him, remove him from the tub, and towel him as dry as possible. To avoid getting an impromptu bath yourself, you must act quickly, for once he is out of the tub, the dog will instinctively shake himself.

While the hair is still slightly damp, use a clean comb or brush to remove any tangles. If the hair is allowed to dry first, it may be completely impossible to remove them.

So far as routine grooming is concerned, the dog's eyes require little attention. Some dogs have a slight accumulation of mucus in the corner of the eyes upon waking mornings. A salt solution (1 teaspoon of table salt to one pint of warm, sterile water) can be sponged around the eyes to remove the stain. During grooming sessions it is well to inspect the eyes, since many breeds are prone to eye injury. Eye problems of a minor nature may be treated at home (see page 50), but it is imperative that any serious eye abnormality be called to the attention of the veterinarian immediately.

Feeding hard dog biscuits and hard bones helps to keep tooth surfaces clean. Slight discoloration may be readily removed by rubbing with a damp cloth dipped in salt or baking soda. The dog's head should be held firmly, the lips pulled apart gently, and the teeth rubbed lightly with the dampened cloth. Regular

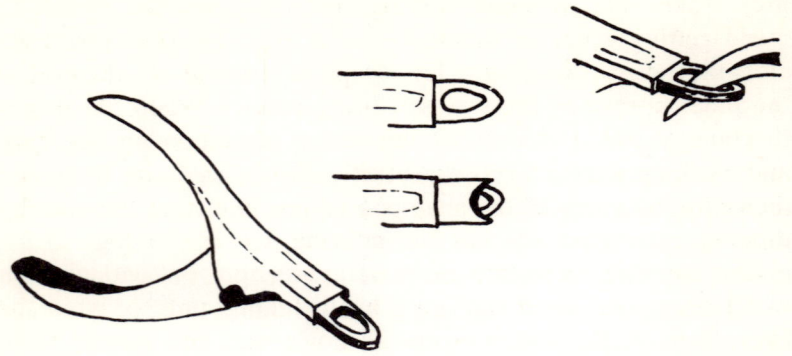

Nail trimmer—center detail shows blade cutting action. Right shows manner of inserting nail in cutter.

care usually keeps the teeth in good condition, but if tartar accumulates, it should be removed by a veterinarian.

If the dog doesn't keep his nails worn down through regular exercise on hard surfaces, they must be trimmed at intervals, for nails that are too long may cause the foot to spread and thus spoil the dog's gait. Neglected nails may even grow so long that they will grow into a circle and puncture the dog's skin. Nails can be cut easily with a nail trimmer that slides over the nail end. The cut is made just outside the faintly pink bloodline that can be seen on white nails. In pigmented nails, the bloodline is not easily seen, so the cut should be made just outside the hooklike projection on the underside of the nails. A few downward strokes with a nail file will smooth the cut surface, and, once shortened, nails can be kept short by filing at regular intervals.

Care must be taken that nails are not cut too short, since blood vessels may be accidentally severed. Should you accidentally cut a nail so short that it bleeds, apply a mild antiseptic and keep the dog quiet until bleeding stops. Usually, only a few drops of blood will be lost. But once a dog's nails have been cut painfully short, he will usually object when his feet are handled.

Nutrition

The main food elements required by dogs are proteins, fats, and carbohydrates. Vitamins A, B complex, D, and E are essential, as are ample amounts of calcium and iron. Nine other minerals are required in small amounts but are amply provided in almost any diet, so there is no need to be concerned about them.

The most important nutrient is protein and it must be provided every day of the dog's life, for it is essential for normal daily growth and replacement of body tissues burned up in daily activity. Preferred animal protein products are beef, mutton, horse meat, and boned fish. Visceral organs—heart, liver, and tripe—are good but if used in too large quantities may cause diarrhea (bones in large amounts have the same effect). Pork, particularly fat pork, is undesirable. The "meat meal" used in some commercial foods is made from scrap meat processed at high temperatures and then dried. It is not quite so nutritious as fresh meat, but in combination with other protein products, it is an acceptable ingredient in the dog's diet.

Cooked eggs and raw egg yolk are good sources of protein, but raw egg white should never be fed since it cannot be digested by the dog and may cause diarrhea. Cottage cheese and milk (fresh, dried, and canned) are high in protein, also. Puppies thrive on milk and it can well be included in the diet of older dogs, too, if mixed with meat, vegetables, and meal. Soy-bean meal, wheat germ meal, and dried brewers yeast are vegetable products high in protein and may be used to advantage in the diet.

Vegetable and animal fats in moderate amounts should be used, especially if a main ingredient of the diet is dry or kibbled food. Fats should not be used excessively or the dog may become overweight. Generally, fats should be increased slightly in the winter and reduced somewhat during warm weather.

Carbohydrates are required for proper assimilation of fats. Dog biscuits, kibble, dog meal, and other dehydrated foods are good sources of carbohydrates, as are cereal products derived from rice, corn, wheat, and ground or rolled oats.

Vegetables supply additional proteins, vitamins, and minerals, and by providing bulk are of value in overcoming constipation. Raw or cooked carrots, celery, lettuce, beets, asparagus, tomatoes, and cooked spinach may be used. They should always be chopped or ground well and mixed with the other food. Various combinations may be used, but a good home-mixed ration for the mature dog consists of two parts of meat and one each of vegetables and dog meal (or cereal product).

Dicalcium phosphate and cod-liver oil are added to puppy diets to ensure inclusion of adequate amounts of calcium and Vitamins A and D. Indiscriminate use of dietary supplements is not only unjustified but may actually be harmful and many breeders feel that their over-use in diets of extremely small breeds may lead to excessive growth as well as to overweight at maturity.

Foods manufactured by well-known and reputable food processors are nutritionally sound and are offered in sufficient variety of flavors, textures, and consistencies that most dogs will find them tempting and satisfying. Canned foods are usually "ready to eat," while dehydrated foods in the form of kibble, meal, or biscuits may require the addition of water or milk. Dried foods containing fat sometimes become rancid, so to avoid an unpalatable change in flavor, the manufacturer may not include fat in dried food but recommend its addition at the time the water or milk is added.

Candy and other sweets are taboo, for the dog has no nutritional need for them and if he is permitted to eat them, he will usually eat less of foods he requires. Also taboo are fried foods, highly seasoned foods and extremely starchy foods, for the dog's digestive tract is not equipped to handle them.

Frozen foods should be thawed completely and warmed at least to lukewarm, while hot foods should be cooled to lukewarm. Food should be in a fairly firm state, for sloppy food is difficult for the dog to digest.

Whether meat is raw or cooked makes little difference, so long as the dog is also given the juice that seeps from the meat during cooking. Bones provide little nourishment, although gnawing bones helps make the teeth strong and helps to keep tartar from accumulating on them. Beef bones, especially large knuckle bones, are best. Fish, poultry, and chop bones should never be given to dogs since they have a tendency to splinter and may puncture the dog's digestive tract.

Clean, fresh, cool water is essential to all dogs and an adequate supply should be readily available twenty-four hours a day from the time the puppy is big enough to walk. Especially during hot weather, the drinking pan should be emptied and refilled at frequent intervals.

Puppies usually are weaned by the time they are six weeks old, so when you acquire a new puppy ten to twelve weeks old, he will already have been started on a feeding schedule. The breeder should supply exact details as to number of meals per day, types and amounts of food offered, etc. It is essential to adhere to this established routine, for drastic changes in diet may produce intestinal upsets.

Until a puppy is six months old, milk formula is an integral part of the diet. A day's supply should be made up at one time and stored in the refrigerator, and the quantity needed for each meal warmed at feeding time. The following combination is good for all breeds:

1 pint whole fresh milk	1 tablespoon lime water
1 raw egg yolk, slightly beaten	1 tablespoon lactose

The two latter items (as well as cod-liver oil and dicalcium phosphate to be added to solid food) are readily available at pet supply stores and drug stores.

At twelve weeks of age the amount of formula given at each feeding will vary from three to four tablespoonfuls for the Toy breeds, to perhaps two cupfuls for the large breeds. If the puppy is on the five-meal-a-day schedule when he leaves the kennel, three of the meals (first, third, and fifth each day) should consist of formula only. On a four-meal schedule, the first and fourth meals should be formula.

In either case, the second meal of the day should consist of chopped beef (preferably raw). The amount needed will vary from about three tablespoonfuls for Toy breeds up to one-half cupful for large breeds. The other meal should consist of equal parts of chopped beef and strained, cooked vegetables to which is added a little dry toast. (If you plan eventually to feed your dog canned food or dog meal, it can gradually be introduced at this meal.) Cod-liver oil and dicalcium phosphate should be mixed with the food for this meal. The amount of each will vary from one-half teaspoonful for Toys to 1 tablespoonful for large breeds.

The amount of food offered at each meal must gradually be increased and by five months the puppy will require about twice what he needed at three months. Puppies should be fat, and it is best to let them eat as much as they want at each meal, so long as they are hungry again when it is time for the next feeding. Any food not eaten within fifteen minutes should be taken away. With a little attention to the dog's eating habits, the owner can prepare enough food and still not waste any.

When the puppy is five months old, the final feeding of the day can be eliminated and the five meals compressed into four so the puppy still receives the same quantities and types of food. At six or seven months, the four meals can be compressed into three. By the time a puppy of small or medium breed is eleven to twelve months old, feedings can be reduced to two meals a day. At the end of the first year, cod-liver oil and dicalcium phosphate can usually be discontinued.

Large breeds mature more slowly and three meals a day are usually necessary until eighteen or twenty-four months of age. Cod-liver oil and dicalcium phosphate should be continued, too, until the large dog reaches maturity.

A mature dog usually eats slightly less than he did as a growing puppy. For mature dogs, one large meal a day is usually sufficient, although some owners prefer to give two meals. As long as the dog enjoys optimum health and is neither too fat nor too thin, the number of meals a day makes little difference.

The amount of food required for mature dogs will vary. With canned dog food or home-prepared foods (that is, the combination of meat, vegetables, and meal), the approximate amount required is one-half ounce of food per pound of body weight. Thus, about eight ounces of such foods would be needed each day for a mature dog weighing sixteen pounds. If the dog is fed a dehydrated commercial food, approximately one ounce of food is needed for each pound of body weight. Approximately one pound of dry food per day would be required by a dog weighing sixteen pounds. Most manufacturers of commercial foods provide information on packages as to approximate daily needs of various breeds.

As a dog becomes older and less active, he may become too fat. Or his appetite may decrease so he becomes too thin. It is necessary to adjust the diet in either case, for the dog will live longer and enjoy better health if he is maintained in trim condition. The simplest way to decrease or increase body weight is by decreasing or increasing the amount of fat in the diet. Protein content should be maintained at a high level throughout the dog's life, although the amount of food at each meal can be decreased if the dog becomes too fat.

If the older dog becomes reluctant to eat, it may be necessary to coax him with special food he normally relishes. Warming the food will increase its aroma and usually will help to entice the dog to eat. If he still refuses, rubbing some of the food on the dog's lips and gums may stimulate interest. It may be helpful also to offer food in smaller amounts and increase the number of meals per day. Foods that are highly nutritious and easily digested are especially desirable for older dogs. Small amounts of cooked, ground liver, cottage cheese, or mashed, hard-cooked eggs should be included in the diet often.

Before a bitch is bred, her owner should make sure that she is in optimum condition—slightly on the lean side rather than fat. The bitch in whelp is given much the same diet she was fed prior to breeding, with slight increases in amounts of meat, liver, and dairy products. Beginning about six weeks after breeding, she should be fed two meals per day rather than one, and the total daily intake increased. (Some bitches in whelp require as much as 50% more food than they consume normally.) She must not be permitted to become fat, for whelping problems are more likely to occur in overweight dogs. Cod-liver oil and dicalcium phosphate should be provided until after the puppies are weaned. The amount of each will vary from one-half teaspoonful to one tablespoonful a day, depending upon her size.

The dog used only occasionally for breeding will not require a special diet, but he should be well fed and maintained in optimum condition. A dog that is at public stud and used frequently may require a slightly increased amount of food. But his basic diet will require no change so long as his general health is good and his flesh is firm and hard.

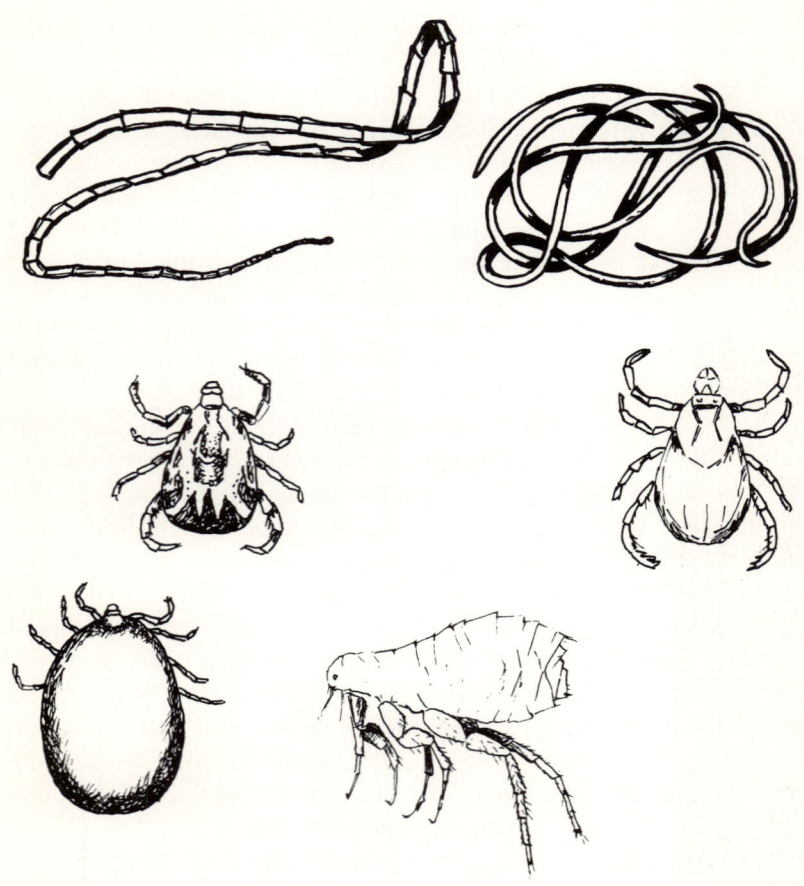

Some common internal and external parasites.

(UPPER LEFT) Tape worm. (UPPER RIGHT) Round worms. (CENTER) American dog ticks—left, female and right, male (much enlarged). (LOWER LEFT) Female tick engorged. (LOWER RIGHT) dog flea (much enlarged).

Maintaining the Dog's Health

Proper nutrition is essential in maintaining the dog's resistance to infectious diseases, in reducing susceptibility to organic diseases, and, of course, in preventing dietary deficiency diseases.

Rickets is probably the most common deficiency disease and afflicts puppies not provided sufficient calcium and Vitamin D. Bones fail to calcify properly, development of teeth is retarded, joints become knobby and deformed, and muscles are flabby. Symptoms include lameness, arching of neck and back, and a tendency of the legs to bow. Treatment consists of providing adequate amounts of dicalcium phosphate and Vitamin D and exposing the dog to sunlight. If detected and treated before reaching an advanced stage, bone damage may be lessened somewhat, although it cannot be corrected completely.

Osteomalacia, similar to rickets, may occur in adult dogs. Treatment is the same as for rickets, but here, too, prevention is preferable to cure. Permanent deformities resulting from rickets or osteomalacia will not be inherited, so once victims recover, they can be used for breeding.

To prevent the growth of disease-producing bacteria and other micro-organisms, cleanliness is essential. All equipment, especially water and food dishes, must be kept immaculately clean. Cleanliness is also essential in controlling external parasites, which thrive in unsanitary surroundings.

Fleas, lice, mites, and ticks can be eradicated in the dog's quarters by regular use of one of the insecticide sprays with a four to six weeks' residual effect. Bedding, blankets, and pillows should be laundered frequently and treated with an insecticide containing rotenone or DDT. Treatment for external parasites varies, depending upon the parasite involved, but a number of good dips and powders are available at pet stores.

Fleas may be eliminated by using a flea powder containing lindane. The coat must be dusted thoroughly with the powder at frequent intervals during the summer months when fleas are a problem. For eradicating lice, dips containing rotenone or DDT must be applied to the coat. A fine-toothed comb should then be used to remove dead lice and eggs, which are firmly attached to the coat. Mites live deep in the ear canal, producing irritation to the lining of the ear and causing a brownish-black, dry type discharge. Plain mineral oil or ear ointment should be swabbed on the inner surface of the ear twice a week until mites are eliminated. Ticks may carry Rocky Mountain spotted fever, so, to avoid possible infection, they should be removed from the dog only with tweezers and should be destroyed by burning (or by dropping them into insecticide). Heavy infestation can be controlled by sponging the coat daily with a solution containing a special tick dip.

Among preparations available for controlling parasites on the dog's body are some that can be given internally. Since dosage must be carefully controlled, these preparations should not be used without consulting a veterinarian.

Internal parasites, with the exception of the tapeworm, may be transmitted from a mother dog to the puppies. Infestation may also result from contact with infected bedding or through access to a yard where an infected dog relieves himself. The types that may infest dogs are roundworms, whipworms, tapeworms, hookworms, and heartworms. All cause similar symptoms: a generally unthrifty appearance, stary coat, dull eyes, weakness and emaciation despite a ravenous appetite, coughing, vomiting, diarrhea, and sometimes bloody stools. Not all symptoms are present in every case, of course.

Promiscuous dosing for worms is dangerous and different types of worms require different treatment. So if you suspect your dog has worms, ask your veterinarian to make a microscopic examination of the feces, and to prescribe appropriate treatment if evidence of worm infestation is found.

Clogged anal glands cause intense discomfort, which the dog may attempt to relieve by scooting himself along the floor on his haunches. These glands, located on either side of the anus, secrete a substance that enables the dog to expel the contents of the rectum. If they become clogged, they may give the dog an unpleasant odor and when neglected, serious infection may result. Contents of the glands can be easily expelled into a wad of

cotton, which should be held under the tail with the left hand. Then, using the right hand, pressure should be exerted with the thumb on one side of the anus, the forefinger on the other. The normal secretion is brownish in color, with an unpleasant odor. The presence of blood or pus indicates infection and should be called to the attention of a veterinarian.

Fits, often considered a symptom of worms, may result from a variety of causes, including vitamin deficiencies, or playing to the point of exhaustion. A veterinarian should be consulted when a fit occurs, for it may be a symptom of serious illness.

Distemper takes many and varied forms, so it is sometimes difficult for even experienced veterinarians to diagnose. It is the number one killer of dogs, and although it is not unknown in older dogs, its victims are usually puppies. While some dogs do recover, permanent damage to the brain or nervous system is often sustained. Symptoms may include lethargy, diarrhea, vomiting, reduced appetite, cough, nasal discharge, inflammation of the eyes, and a rise in temperature. If distemper is suspected, a veterinarian must be consulted at once, for early treatment is essential. Effective preventive measures lie in inoculation. Shots for temporary immunity should be given all puppies within a few weeks after whelping, and the permanent inoculations should be given as soon thereafter as possible.

Hardpad has been fairly prevalent in Great Britain for a number of years, and its incidence in the United States is increasing. Symptoms are similar to those of distemper, but as the disease progresses, the pads of the feet harden and eventually peel. Chances of recovery are not favorable unless prompt veterinary care is secured.

Infectious hepatitis in dogs affects the liver, as does the human form, but apparently is not transmissible to man. Symptoms are similar to those of distemper, and the disease rapidly reaches the acute stage. Since hepatitis is often fatal, prompt veterinary treatment is essential. Effective vaccines are available and should be provided all puppies. A combination distemper-hepatitis vaccine is sometimes used.

Leptospirosis is caused by a micro-organism often transmitted by contact with rats, or by ingestion of food contaminated by rats. The disease can be transmitted to man, so anyone caring for an afflicted dog must take steps to avoid infection. Symptoms include vomiting, loss of appetite, diarrhea, fever, depression and lethargy, redness of eyes and gums, and sometimes jaundice. Since permanent kidney damage may result, veterinary treatment should be secured immediately.

Rabies is a disease that is always fatal—and it is transmissible to man. It is caused by a virus that attacks the nervous system and is present in the saliva of an infected animal. When an infected animal bites another, the virus is transmitted to the new victim. It may also enter the body through cuts and scratches that come in contact with saliva containing the virus.

All warm-blooded animals are subject to rabies and it may be transmitted by foxes, skunks, squirrels, horses, and cattle as well as dogs. Anyone bitten by a dog (or other animal) should see his physician immediately, and health and law enforcement officials should be notified. Also, if your dog is bitten by another animal, consult your veterinarian immediately.

In most areas, rabies shots are required by law. Even if not required, all dogs should be given anti-rabies vaccine, for it is an effective preventive measure.

Injuries of a serious nature—deep cuts, broken bones, severe burns, etc.—always require veterinary care. However, the dog may need first aid before being moved to a veterinary hospital.

A dog injured in any way should be approached cautiously, for reactions of a dog in pain are unpredictable and he may bite even a beloved master. A muzzle should always be applied before any attempt is made to move the dog or treat him in any way. The muzzle can be improvised from a strip of cloth, bandage, or even heavy cord, looped firmly around the dog's jaws and tied under the lower jaw. The ends should then be extended back of the neck and tied again so the loop around the jaws will stay in place.

A stretcher for moving a heavy dog can be improvised from a rug or board—preferably two people should be available to transport it. A small dog can be carried by one person simply by grasping the loose skin at the nape of the neck with one hand and placing the other hand under the dog's hips.

Severe bleeding from a leg can be controlled by applying a tourniquet between the wound and the body, but the tourniquet must be loosened at ten-minute intervals. Severe bleeding from head or body can be controlled by placing a cloth or gauze pad over the wound, then applying firm pressure with the hand.

To treat minor cuts, first trim the hair from around the wound, then wash the area with warm soapy water and apply a mild antiseptic such as tincture of metaphen.

Shock is usually the aftermath of severe injury and requires immediate veterinary attention. The dog appears dazed, lips and tongue are pale, and breathing is shallow. The dog should be wrapped in blankets and kept warm, and if possible, kept lying down with his head lower than his body.

Fractures require immediate professional attention. A broken bone should be immobilized while the dog is transported to the veterinarian but no attempt should be made to splint it.

Burns from hot liquid or hot metals should be treated by applying a bland ointment, provided the burned area is small. Burns over large areas should be treated by a veterinarian.

Burns from chemicals should first be treated by flushing the coat with plain water, taking care to protect the dog's eyes and ears. A baking soda solution can then be applied to neutralize the chemical further. If the burned area is small, a bland ointment should be applied. If the burned area is large, more extensive treatment will be required, as well as veterinary care.

Poisoning is more often accidental than deliberate, but whichever the case, symptoms and treatment are the same. If the poisoning is not discovered immediately, the dog may be found unconscious. His mouth will be slimy, he will tremble, have difficulty breathing, and possibly go into convulsions. Veterinary treatment must be secured immediately.

If you find the dog eating something you know to be poisonous, induce vomiting immediately by repeatedly forcing the dog to swallow a mixture of equal parts of hydrogen peroxide and water. Delay of even a few minutes may result in death. When the contents of the stomach have been emptied, force the dog to swallow raw egg white, which will slow absorption of the poison. Then call the veterinarian. Provide him with information as to the type of poison, and follow his advice as to further treatment.

Some chemicals are toxic even though not swallowed, so before using a product, make sure it can be used safely around pets.

Electric shock usually results because an owner negligently leaves an electric cord exposed where the dog can chew on it. If possible, disconnect the cord before touching the dog. Otherwise, yank the cord from the dog's mouth so you will not receive a shock when you try to help him. If the dog is unconscious, artificial respiration and stimulants will be required, so a veterinarian should be consulted at once.

Eye problems of a minor nature—redness or occasional discharge—may be treated with a few drops of boric acid solution (2%) or salt solution (1 teaspoonful table salt to 1 pint sterile water). Cuts on the eyeball, bruises close to the eyes, or persistent discharge shoud be treated only by a veterinarian.

Skin problems usually cause persistent itching. However, *follicular mange* does not usually do so but is evidenced by moth-eaten-looking patches, especially about the head and along the back. *Sarcoptic mange* produces severe itching and is evidenced by patchy, crusty areas on body, legs, and abdomen. Any evidence suggesting either should be called to the attention of a veterinarian. Both require extensive treatment and both may be contracted by humans.

Eczema is characterized by extreme itching, redness of the skin and exudation of serous matter. It may result from a variety of causes, and the exact cause in a particular case may be difficult to determine. Relief may be secured by dusting the dog twice a week with a soothing powder containing a fungicide and an insecticide.

Allergies are not readily distinguished from other skin troubles except through laboratory tests. However, dog owners should be alert to the fact that straw, shavings, or newspapers used for bedding, various coat dressings and shampoos, or simply bathing the dog too often, may produce allergic skin reactions in some dogs. Thus, a change in dog-keeping practices often relieves them.

Symptoms of illness may be so obvious there is no question that the dog is ill, or so subtle that the owner isn't sure whether there is a change from normal or not. *Loss of appetite, malaise* (general lack of interest in what is going on), *and vomiting* may be ignored if they occur singly and persist only for a day. However, in combination with other evidence of illness, such symptoms may be significant and the dog should be watched closely. *Abnormal bowel movements,* especially diarrhea or bloody stools, are cause for immediate concern. *Urinary abnormalities* may indicate infections, and bloody urine is always an indication of a serious condition. When a dog that has long been housebroken suddenly becomes incontinent, a veterinarian should be consulted, for he may be able to suggest treatment or medication that will be helpful.

Persistent coughing is often considered a symptom of worms, but may also indicate heart trouble—especially in older dogs.

Vomiting is another symptom often attributed to worm infestation. Dogs suffering from indigestion sometimes eat grass, apparently to induce vomiting and relieve discomfort.

Stary coat—dull and lackluster—indicates generally poor health and possible worm infestation. *Dull eyes* may result from similar conditions. Certain forms of blindness may also cause the eyes to lose the sparkle of vibrant good health.

Fever is a positive indication of illness and consistent deviation from the normal temperature range of 100 to 102 degrees is cause for concern. To take the dog's temperature, first place the dog on his side. Coat the bulb of a rectal thermometer with petroleum jelly, raise the dog's tail, insert the thermometer to approximately half its length, and hold it in position for two minutes. Clean the thermometer with rubbing alcohol after each use and be sure to shake it down.

A dog that is seriously ill, requiring surgical treatment, transfusions, or intravenous feeding, must be hospitalized. One requiring less complicated treatment is better cared for at home, but it is essential that the dog be kept in a quiet environment. Preferably, his bed should be in a room apart from family activity, yet close at hand, so his condition can be checked frequently. Clean bedding and adequate warmth are essential, as are a constant supply of fresh, cool water, and foods to tempt the appetite.

Special equipment is not ordinarily needed, but the following items will be useful in caring for a sick dog, as well as in giving first aid for injuries:

petroleum jelly	tincture of metaphen
rubbing alcohol	cotton, gauze, and adhesive tape
mineral oil	burn ointment
rectal thermometer	tweezers
hydrogen peroxide	boric acid solution (2%)

If special medication is prescribed, it may be administered in any one of several ways. A pill or small capsule may be concealed in a small piece of meat, which the dog will usually swallow with no problem. A large capsule may be given by holding the dog's mouth open, inserting the capsule as far as possible down the throat, then holding the mouth closed until the dog swallows. Liquid medicine should be measured into a small bottle or test tube. Then, if the corner of the dog's lip is pulled out while the head is tilted upward, the liquid can be poured between the lips and teeth, a small amount at a time. If he refuses to swallow, keeping the dog's head tilted and stroking his throat will usually induce swallowing.

Foods offered the sick dog should be particularly nutritious and easily digested. Meals should be smaller than usual and offered at more frequent intervals. If the dog is reluctant to eat, offer food he particularly likes and warm it slightly to increase aroma and thus make it more tempting.

Housing Your Dog

Every dog should have a bed of his own, snug and warm, where he can retire undisturbed when he wishes to nap. And, especially with a small puppy, it is desirable to have the bed arranged so the dog can be securely confined at times, safe and contented. If the puppy is taught early in life to stay quietly in his box at night, or when the family is out, the habit will carry over into adulthood and will benefit both dog and master.

The dog should never be banished to a damp, cold basement, but should be quartered in an out-of-the-way corner close to the center of family activity. His bed can be an elaborate cushioned affair with electric warming pad, or simply a rectangular wooden box or heavy paper carton, cushioned with a clean cotton rug or towel. Actually, the latter is ideal for a new puppy, for it is snug, easy to clean, and expendable. A "door" can be cut on one side of the box for easy access, but it should be placed in such a way that the dog can still be confined when desirable.

The shipping crates used by professional handlers at dog shows make ideal indoor quarters. They are lightweight but strong, provide adequate air circulation, yet are snug and warm and easily cleaned. For the dog owner who takes his dog along when he travels, a dog crate is ideal, for the dog will willingly stay in his accustomed bed during long automobile trips, and the crate can be taken inside motels or hotels at night, making the dog a far more acceptable guest.

Dog crates are made of chromed metal or wood, and some have tops covered with a special rubber matting so they can be used as grooming tables. Anyone moderately handy with tools can construct a crate similar to the one illustrated on page 35.

Crates come in various sizes, to suit various breeds of dogs. For reasons of economy, the size selected for a puppy should be adequate for use when the dog is full grown. If the area seems too large when the puppy is small, a temporary cardboard partition can be installed to limit the area he occupies.

The dog owner who lives in the suburbs or in the country may want to keep a mature dog outdoors part of the time, in which case an outdoor doghouse should be provided. This type of kennel can also be constructed by the home handyman, but must be more substantial than quarters used indoors.

Outside finish of the doghouse can be of any type, but double wall construction will make for greater warmth in chilly weather. The floor should be smooth and easy to clean, so tongued and grooved boards or plywood are best. To keep the floor from contact with the damp earth, supports should be laid flat on the ground, running lengthwise of the structure. 2 x 4s serve well as supports for doghouses for small or medium breeds, but 4 x 4s should be used for large breeds.

The outdoor kennel must be big enough so that the dog can turn around inside, but small enough so that his body heat will keep it warm in chilly weather. The overall length of the kennel shoud be twice the length of the adult dog, measured from tip of nose to onset of tail. Width of the structure should be approximately three-fourths the length. And height from the floor to the point where the roof begins should be approximately one and a half the adult dog's height at the shoulders. If you build the house when the dog is still a puppy, you can determine his approximate adult size by referring to the Standard for his breed.

An "A" type roof is preferable, and an overhang of six inches all the way around will provide protection from sun and rain. If the roof is hinged to fold back, the interior of the kennel can be cleaned readily.

The entrance should be placed to one side rather than in the center, which will provide further protection against the weather. One of the commercially made door closures of rubber will keep out rain, snow, and wind, yet give the pet complete freedom to enter and leave his home.

The best location for the doghouse is where it will get enough morning sun to keep it dry, yet will not be in full sun during hot afternoons. If possible, the back of the doghouse should be placed toward the prevailing winds.

A fenced run or yard is essential to the outdoor kennel, and the fence must be sturdy enough that the dog cannot break through it, and high enough so he cannot jump or climb over it. The gate should have a latch of a type that can't be opened accidentally. The area enclosed must provide the dog with space to exercise freely, or else the dog must be exercised on the leash every day, for no dog should be confined to a tiny yard day after day without adequate exercise.

The yard must be kept clean and odor free, and the doghouse must be scrubbed and disinfected at frequent intervals. One of the insecticides made especially for use in kennels—one with a four to six weeks' residual effect—should be used regularly on floors and walls, inside and out.

Enough bedding must be provided so the dog can snuggle into it and keep warm in chilly weather. Bedding should either be of a type that is inexpensive, so it can be discarded and replaced frequently, or of a type that can be laundered readily. Dogs are often allergic to fungi found on straw, hay, or grass, and sometimes newspaper ink, but cedar shavings and old cotton rugs and blankets usually serve very well.

The Stone-age Dog

A Spotted Dog from India, "Parent of the Modern Coach dog."

History of
the Genus Canis

The history of man's association with the dog is a fascinating one, extending into the past at least seventy centuries, and involving the entire history of civilized man from the early Stone Age to the present.

The dog, technically a member of the genus *Canis,* belongs to the zoological family group *Canidae,* which also includes such animals as wolves, foxes, jackals, and coyotes. In the past it was generally agreed that the dog resulted from the crossing of various members of the family *Canidae*. Recent findings have amended this theory somewhat, and most authorities now feel the jackal probably has no direct relationship with the dog. Some believe dogs are descended from wolves and foxes, with the wolf the main progenitor. As evidence, they cite the fact that the teeth of the wolf are identical in every detail with those of the dog, whereas the teeth of the jackal are totally different.

Still other authorities insist that the dog always has existed as a separate and distinct animal. This group admits that it is possible for a dog to mate with a fox, coyote, or wolf, but points out that the resulting puppies are unable to breed with each other, although they can breed with stock of the same genus as either parent. Therefore, they insist, it was impossible for a new and distinct genus to have developed from such crossings. They then cite the fact that any dog can be mated with any other dog and the progeny bred among themselves. These researchers point out, too, heritable characteristics that are totally different in the three animals. For instance, the pupil of the dog's eye is round, that of the wolf oblique, and that of the jackal vertical. Tails, too, differ considerably, for tails of foxes, coyotes, and wolves always drop behind them, while those of dogs may be carried over the back or straight up.

Much conjecture centers on two wild dog species that still exist—the Dingo of Australia, and the Dhole in India. Similar in appearance, both are reddish in color, both have rather long, slender jaws, both have rounded ears that stand straight up, and both species hunt in packs. Evidence indicates that they had the same ancestors. Yet, today, they live in areas that are more than 4,000 miles apart.

Despite the fact that it is impossible to determine just when the dog first appeared as a distinct species, archeologists have found definite proof that the dog was the first animal domesticated by man. When man lived by tracking, trapping, and killing game, the dog added to the forces through which man discovered and captured the quarry. Man shared his primitive living quarters with the dog, and the two together devoured the prey. Thus, each helped to sustain the life of the other. The dog assisted man, too, by defending the campsite against marauders. As man gradually became civilized, the dog's usefulness was extended to guarding the other animals man domesticated, and, even before the wheel was invented, the dog served as a beast of burden. In fact, archeological findings show that aboriginal peoples of Switzerland and Ireland used the dog for such purposes long before they learned to till the soil.

Cave drawings from the palaeolithic era, which was the earliest part of the Old World Stone Age, include hunting scenes in which a rough, canine-like form is shown alongside huntsmen. One of these drawings is believed to be 50,000 years old, and gives credence to the theory that all dogs are descended from a primitive type ancestor that was neither fox nor wolf.

Archeological findings show that Europeans of the New Stone Age possessed a breed of dogs of wolf-like appearance, and a similar breed has been traced through the successive Bronze Age and Iron Age. Accurate details are not available, though, as to the external appearance of domesticated dogs prior to historic times (roughly four to five thousand years ago).

Early records in Chaldean and Egyptian tombs show that several distinct and well-established dog types had been developed by about 3700 B.C. Similar records show that the early people of the Nile Valley regarded the dog as a god, often burying it as a mummy in special cemeteries and mourning its death.

Some of the early Egyptian dogs had been given names, such as Akna, Tarn, and Abu, and slender dogs of the Greyhound type and a short-legged Terrier type are depicted in drawings found

Bas-relief of Hunters with Nets and Mastiffs. From the walls of Assurbanipal's palace at Nineveh 668-626 B.C. *British Museum.*

in Egyptian royal tombs that are at least 5,000 years old. The Afghan Hound and the Saluki are shown in drawings of only slightly later times. Another type of ancient Egyptian dog was much heavier and more powerful, with short coat and massive head. These probably hunted by scent, as did still another type of Egyptian dog that had a thick furry coat, a tail curled almost flat over the back, and erect "prick" ears.

Early Romans and Greeks mentioned their dogs often in literature, and both made distinctions between those that hunted by sight and those that hunted by scent. The Romans' canine classifications were similar to those we use now. In addition to dogs comparable to the Greek sight and scent hounds, the ancient Romans had Canes *villatici* (housedogs) and Canes *pastorales* (sheepdogs), corresponding to our present-day working dogs.

The dog is mentioned many times in the Old Testament. The first reference, in Genesis, leads some Biblical scholars to assert that man and dog have been companions from the time man was created. And later Biblical references bring an awareness of the diversity in breeds and types existing thousands of years ago.

As civilization advanced, man found new uses for dogs. Some required great size and strength. Others needed less of these characteristics but greater agility and better sight. Still others needed an accentuated sense of smell. As time went on, men kept those puppies that suited specific purposes especially well and bred them together. Through ensuing generations of selective breeding, desirable characteristics appeared with increasing frequency. Dogs used in a particular region for a special purpose gradually became more like each other, yet less like dogs of other areas used for different purposes. Thus were established the foundations for the various breeds we have today.

The American Kennel Club, the leading dog organization in the United States, divides the various breeds into six "Groups," based on similarity of purposes for which they were developed.

"Sporting Dogs" include the Pointers, Setters, Spaniels, and Retrievers that were developed by sportsmen interested in hunting game birds. Most of the Pointers and Setters are of comparatively recent origin. Their development parallels the development of sporting firearms, and most of them evolved in the British Isles. Exceptions are the Weimaraner, which was developed in Germany, and the Vizsla, or Hungarian Pointer, believed to have been developed by the Magyar hordes that swarmed over Central Europe a thousand years ago. The Irish were among the first to use Spaniels, though the name indicates that the original stock may have come from Spain. Two Sporting breeds, the American Water Spaniel, and the Chesapeake Bay Retriever, were developed entirely in the United States.

"Hounds," among which are Dachshunds, Beagles, Bassets, Harriers, and Foxhounds, are used singly, in pairs, or in packs to "course" (or run) and hunt for rabbits, foxes, and various rodents. But little larger, the Norwegian Elkhound is used in its native country to hunt big game—moose, bear, and deer.

The smaller Hound breeds hunt by scent, while the Irish Wolfhound, Borzoi, Scottish Deerhound, Saluki, and Greyhound hunt by sight. The Whippet, Saluki, and Greyhound are notably fleet of foot, and racing these breeds (particularly the Greyhound) is popular sport.

The Bloodhound is a member of the Hound Group that is known world-wide for its scenting ability. On the other hand, the Basenji is a comparatively rare Hound breed and has the distinction of being the only dog that cannot bark.

"Working Dogs" have the greatest utilitarian value of all modern dogs and contribute to man's welfare in diverse ways. The Boxer, Doberman Pinscher, Rottweiler, German Shepherd, Great Dane, and Giant Schnauzer are often trained to serve as sentries and aid police in patrolling streets. The German Shepherd is especially noted as a guide dog for the blind. The Collie, the various breeds of Sheepdogs, and the two Corgi breeds are known throughout the world for their extraordinary herding ability. And the exploits of the St. Bernard and Newfoundland are legendary, their records for saving lives unsurpassed.

The Siberian Husky and the Alaskan Malamute are noted for tremendous strength and stamina. Had it not been for these hardy Northern breeds, the great polar expeditions might never have taken place, for Admiral Byrd used these dogs to reach points inaccessible by other means. Even today, with our jet-age transportation, the Northern breeds provide a more practical means of travel in frigid areas than do modern machines.

"Terriers" derive their name from the Latin *terra,* meaning

1. The Newfoundland. 2. The English Setter. 3. The Large Water-spaniel. 4. The Terrier. 5. The Cur-dog. 6. The Shepherd's Dog. 7. The Bulldog. 8. The Mastiff. 9. The Greenland Dog. 10. The Rought Water-dog. 11. The Small Water-spaniel. 12. The Old English Hound. 13. The Dalmatian or Coach-dog. 14. The Comporter (very much of a Papillon). 15. "Toy Dog, Bottle, Glass, and Pipe." *From a vignette.* 16. The Springer or Cocker. *From Thomas Bewick's "General History of Quadrupeds" (1790).*

"earth," for all of the breeds in this Group are fond of burrowing. Terriers hunt by digging into the earth to rout rodents and fur-bearing animals such as badgers, woodchucks, and otters. Some breeds are expected merely to force the animals from their dens in order that the hunter can complete the capture. Others are expected to find and destroy the prey, either on the surface or under the ground.

Terriers come in a wide variety of sizes, ranging from such large breeds as the Airedale and Kerry Blue to such small ones as the Skye, the Dandie Dinmont, the West Highland White, and the Scottish Terrier. England, Ireland, and Scotland produced most of the Terrier breeds, although the Miniature Schnauzer was developed in Germany.

"Toys," as the term indicates, are small breeds. Although they make little claim to usefulness other than as ideal housepets, Toy dogs develop as much protective instinct as do larger breeds and serve effectively in warning of the approach of strangers.

Origins of the Toys are varied. The Pekingese was developed as the royal dog of China more than two thousand years before the birth of Christ. The Chihuahua, smallest of the Toys, originated in Mexico and is believed to be a descendant of the Techichi, a dog of great religious significance to the Aztecs, while the Italian Greyhound was popular in the days of ancient Pompeii.

"Non-Sporting Dogs" include a number of popular breeds of varying ancestry. The Standard and Miniature Poodles were developed in France for the purpose of retrieving game from water. The Bulldog originated in Great Britain and was bred for the purpose of "baiting" bulls. The Chowchow apparently originated centuries ago in China, for it is pictured in a bas relief dated to the Han dynasty of about 150 B.C.

The Dalmatian served as a carriage dog in Dalmatia, protecting travelers in bandit-infested regions. The Keeshond, recognized as the national dog of Holland, is believed to have originated in the Arctic or possibly the Sub-Arctic. The Schipperke, sometimes erroneously described as a Dutch dog, originated in the Flemish provinces of Belgium. And the Lhasa Apso came from Tibet, where it is known as "Abso Seng Kye," the "Bark Lion Sentinel Dog."

During the thousands of years that man and dog have been closely associated, a strong affinity has been built up between the two. The dog has more than earned his way as a helper, and his faithful, selfless devotion to man is legendary. The ways in which the dog has proved his intelligence, his courage, and his dependability in situations of stress are amply recorded in the countless tales of canine heroism that highlight the pages of history, both past and present.

Dogs in Woodcuts. (1st row) (LEFT) "Maltese dog with shorter hair"; (RIGHT) "Spotted sporting dog trained to catch game"; (2nd row) (LEFT) Sporting white dog; (RIGHT) "Spanish dog with floppy ears": (3rd row) (LEFT) "French dog"; (RIGHT) "Mad dog of Grevinus"; (4th row) (LEFT) Hairy Maltese dog; (RIGHT) "English fighting dog ... of horrid aspect." *From Aldrovandus (1637).*

History of the Miniature Schnauzer

While the dog has served man for milleniums and the Schnauzer has served him for centuries, the Miniature Schnauzer as we know it today has been in existence for only a very short period of time. But interestingly, during this short span of years, strides in establishing the beauty and consistency of the present breed have been astronomical. The Miniature Schnauzer has come from virtual nonexistence in this country at the turn of the century to number five in the 1972 ranking of all-breed popularity.

Schnauzers come in three sizes: the Giant Schnauzer, which measures from 21½ to 25½ inches at the withers; the Standard Schnauzer, which measures from 18 to 21 inches at the withers for males and 17 to 19 inches for females; and the smallest of the three, the Miniature Schnauzer, which measures from 12 to 14 inches. However, the history of all Schnauzers begins with the history of the Standard Schnauzer.

Schnauzer-type dogs can be seen in paintings executed as early as the fifteenth century. Lucas Cranach the Elder, Albrecht Durer, and later, Rembrandt, all depicted them. A 1620 statue called "Night Watchman and His Dog" also incorporates a typical Schnauzer. Undoubtedly these larger dogs were favorites as cattle drovers and guards, and the smaller varieties as ratters and household pets.

In simplified lineage, the early purebred Schnauzers came from the cattle lands of Germany and seem to be a development of crosses between the big black Poodle and the wolf-gray Spitz. Through other crosses, very large specimens developed into the present Giant Schnauzer, and the medium-sized dogs developed into the Standard Schnauzer. These early dogs were referred to as Wire-haired Pinschers (the term "pinscher" meaning "terrier"—terrier coming from the Latin "terrarus" meaning earth), but it was not until the late nineteenth century that systematic, purposeful breeding was in progress and breed Standards were formulated. The dogs were first exhibited in 1879, and the first club dedicated to the development of the breed was formed in 1895 and was called the Pinscher-Klub.

The first German Schnauzer studbooks included references not only to the Standard size Schnauzer, but also to Wire-haired *Miniature*

Pinschers, later to become known as Zwergschnauzers ("zwerg" meaning dwarf and "schnauzer" meaning snout). The earliest registration listed as a Miniature Schnauzer was "Findel," a black bitch whelped in 1888, whose background was given as "unknown." Miniature Schnauzers were first exhibited in German shows in 1899.

Questions as to the roots of Miniature Schnauzer development elicit varied responses. Some breed authorities say that the breed resulted from using only the smallest specimens of Standard Schnauzers for breeding. Others, probably more reasonably, contend that Miniatures were the deliberate result of outcrossing small Standard Schnauzers with Affenpinschers. Because many early registrations offered no parental information, it is difficult to be definitive, but many authorities insist on the natural inclusion of Miniature Pinscher blood, and perhaps some Pomeranian. The early years were unquestionably a time when great breeding experimentation was necessary in order to produce the desired result, and consequently there were confusing, inconclusive records, undefined early bloodlines, and much variation in color, coat, type of ears, and so forth. Of course, as soon as the Miniature Schnauzer was recognized as a distinct breed and type was being established, only "purebreds" were mated.

Without question, the three most important German-owned sires of the first years of the twentieth century were Peter v. Westerberg (all black), Prinz v. Rheinstein (described as black with yellow-gray markings), and Lord, the youngest and lightest of the three. While all were of uncertain pedigree, they exhibited and, more importantly, effectively produced the characteristics that were desired during this early period when efforts were being concentrated on stabilizing the breed. These three dogs are the ancestors of almost all of today's Miniature Schnauzers.

Until 1923 there is no record at all of the Miniature Schnauzer in America. German Miniature Schnauzer lines were becoming well established by that time, and in 1923 two Miniature Schnauzers were brought to the United States from the kennels of Rudolph Krappatsch. Unfortunately, the male died and the bitch's two litters did not carry on. The real credit for lasting breed beginnings in this country must go to Mrs. Marie Slattery (then Mrs. Marie Lewis) of Marienhof Kennels fame, who imported three bitches and one male from Rudolph Krappatsch in 1924. Champion-to-be Amsel von der Cyriaksburg, her two daughters, Lady and Lotte von der Goldbachhohe, and a male arrived to fascinate all who saw them.

The next decade evidenced a minor avalanche of Miniature Schnau-

Best Brace in Show, Canada. Left, Can. Ch. Rosehill Von Meyken. Right, Can. Ch. Rosehill Von Zerna.

Eight Travelmore Schnauzers at the Trenton Show, 1969.

zer imports, but most of these lines became extinct. Amsel remains as the first Miniature Schnauzer shown in the United States and as the dam of the first American-born litter, which was whelped in 1925. Ch. Moses Taylor, Amsel's double grandson, was the first American-bred champion. It is probable that most current American champions can be traced back to Amsel.

When Amsel was being shown in the United States, Miniature Schnauzers were not recognized as a breed and they could not be registered with The American Kennel Club, so they were shown with the Standard Schnauzers (called Wire-haired Pinschers) in the Working Group. Then the A.K.C. ruled that they be shown in the Miscellaneous Class. A parent club, the Wire-haired Pinscher Club of America, founded in 1925, embraced fanciers of both the Standards and the Miniatures.

Recognition was granted and registration first permitted in 1926, and separate classes were first offered at the Combined Terrier Clubs Specialty Show in February 1927. Later, all of the Schnauzers were moved to the Terrier Group, with top awards given to both a Standard and a Miniature. Both of these representatives competed in the Terrier Group until 1931, when new A.K.C. rules allowed only one "Best." However, the A.K.C. reversed this decision in 1933. By 1945, Standard Schnauzers were again transferred to the Working Group, where they rightfully belong. In the interim, the A.K.C. had decided that a specialty club could cover only one breed, and since Miniature and Standard Schnauzers had been registered separately for quite a number of years, the Schnauzer Club of America (as it by then had been named) reorganized in 1933 to form the American Miniature Schnauzer Club and the Standard Schnauzer Club of America.

How painfully unsettling these early years must have been for the breeders and exhibitors; and yet, how rewarding, too, to have had a part in establishing Miniature Schnauzers in America.

Boundless credit is due the pioneers of the breed whose tireless determination and devotion finally made a solid base for the future generations from Amsel and her offspring.

For those who wish to make intensive Miniature Schnauzer lineage investigation, two invaluable sources are commended: Mrs. Anne Paramoure Eskrigge's *The Complete Miniature Schnauzer,* which excels in its detailed sections on breed histories, and John T. Knight's compilation to 1968, "The American Miniature Schnauzer Registration Index." This index is an alphabetical listing of all champion and obedience titled Miniature Schnauzers, plus dogs appearing in their pedigrees back to the first imported dogs. While somewhat time-consuming, it is great fun and a rather awesome experience to trace a Schnauzer's ancestry—in our case, all the way back to Amsel herself, from several directions and many times over.

To say that beauty is in the eyes of the beholder or that form follows function might explain in part the changes in the appearance of the Miniature Schnauzer over the past fifty years. How much change evolved deliberately and how much evolved accidentally can never be determined. How much is structural and how much is surface is open to individual opinion. Trends and tastes change, and, though ever so slowly, the result emerges in a new style animal.

For example, size—that is, height at the withers—has been an "eternal Puck." Twelve inches was the original maximum height for the Miniature variety. Early dogs were measured out if they exceeded the twelve inch mark, while today, they would be measured out if they didn't reach that mark, for the current range is twelve to fourteen inches.

To crop or not to crop is another question that has had varying answers. The Standard forbid cropping between 1930 and 1934. Now one rarely if ever sees an uncropped Miniature Schnauzer in the ring in the United States.

Color? Today's usually distinct dark gray salt and pepper was rare in the thirties, but coat texture was at its best then. Breeders today strive for both the harsh textured coat and the profuse furnishings and beard, which seemed to be lacking in some of the earlier dogs.

Trends toward a more streamlined type emerged in the years approaching the fifties, and the term "Terrier-type," used to describe some Miniature Schnauzers, came into the vocabulary.

If one watches a breed over a period of several years, he will probably note changes in such things as quality of movement, the silhouette, tail carriage, height, and perhaps rib spring—all operating within the bounds of the breed Standard. (In addition, styles of grooming change over the years.) As specific, widespread problem areas develop—such as cowhocks or bad bites—breeders concentrate on correcting them. Other problems may recur or may appear suddenly as recessives. All of this is part of the great challenge of the sport—or the science—the thing that keeps breeders striving for that really sensational specimen, for that really outstanding producer which will create new impact in breed history.

Ch. Deltone Deldomingo, 17 C.C.s, 14 Reserve C.C.s, 14 Bests of Breed.

Can. Ch. Eastwight Sea Voyager, CD, uncropped English import.

The Breed in Other Countries

The Miniature Schnauzer's current popularity is not limited to the United States, for fanciers around the world are equally enthusiastic.

Canada has a small but active Miniature Schnauzer Club which was founded in 1950. Miniature Schnauzers number by far the largest entries in the Terrier Group there, and many American dogs travel to Canada to win a second championship. Several A.K.C. champions also have gained additional titles in Bermuda and Mexico.

In Germany, World War II ended the large number of exports to the United States which had been prevalent prior to that time. German registrations went down and remained down until the early fifties, but by 1967 the breed ranked seventh in popularity in Germany. Interestingly, on the Continent color crosses are not permitted and black and silvers are not recognized, but in England both are acceptable.

Unfortunately, Miniature Schnauzer development in England has been slow and difficult. While the first Schnauzers arrived in 1928, fanciers faced difficulties similar to but more severe than those of the early years in the United States—changes in the name and in the Group placement of the breed, problems of registration, formation of a breed club, and so on. But worst of all, there were problems because of the war, plus the six-month quarantine on imports (both expensive and time-consuming), and a ruling in effect against cropped dogs. Even if the new owner survived all of the obstacles in acquiring a Miniature Schnauzer, he usually couldn't show the import because of the ears.

The Miniature Schnauzer Club of Great Britain (founded in 1953) is now active and thriving despite early setbacks. There are a number of Miniatures in Scotland, and Schnauzer Clubs are active in Italy, Austria, France, Switzerland, Belgium, and Holland. Italy has produced outstanding black Miniatures, and in Australia blacks have been making good records.

Breed Standards vary somewhat in different parts of the world and, frequently, grooming styles differ radically. Also, shows are judged differently. Still, underneath it all, the Miniature Schnauzer is the same dog we admire!

Ch. Carrousel Clarabo and friends.

Marcheim Portrait of Jennie checks out a handbag.

Mr. Dean Jagger and his daughter with Eric of Elfland. 1955. M.G.M. Photo.

Personality of the Miniature Schnauzer

Each Miniature Schnauzer is an individual. His adult personality is a meshing of his heredity and his training, and sometimes it is difficult to distinguish between the two. The characteristics of personality and type place the breed in the Terrier Group of dogs, even though the Miniature Schnauzer is not a true Terrier.

In general, a Miniature Schnauzer is outgoing and alert. He is normally not a hole-digger, howler, nor roamer. However, he is ever-curious and ready for action and might be off in a flash after anything that moves, or that sounds or smells interesting. He is a watch dog that will guard his territory and his family, but he will readily accept strangers when introduced properly. He is good with children when children are good with him. It must be understood that to have all of these virtues, the puppy or grown dog must have been well bred and must have had the proper training and affection to give him security and establish his place in the family. In short, he must have been encouraged to develop his personality to its fullest extent.

Neither shyness nor viciousness are typical of the breed, although bad temper, like predisposition to certain maladies and structural traits, can be inherited. However, if a dog becomes very aggressive, shy, or short-tempered because he has been tormented and teased by humans or dominated by other animals, the dog or his breeding shouldn't be blamed.

Accept the fact that a Miniature Schnauzer is independent and you will find him to be a constant source of amusement and amazement! He thrives on praise and wants to please, but sometimes only on his own terms! In order to work out a happy relationship, the owner must understand his dog and use training techniques that are in accord with the dog's personality. This characteristic of independence gives the Miniature Schnauzer much ability to think for himself.

Your Miniature Schnauzer knows by the clothes you're wearing whether you're going out or staying in. He can distinguish the sound of your car from others and will wait at the door, ready to welcome you. He will comfort you when you're sad and rejoice with you when you're happy. He will stay by a sickbed all day long, or follow your every step. Yet, our matriarch, one of our best trained dogs, will pretend to be deaf, blind, and dumb if she doesn't want to come back into the house on a beautiful, sunny day when she senses that I'm not totally serious about my request!

Though today their major purpose in life is that of devoted house dogs, Miniature Schnauzers were bred and used as ratters and guards in the barns and stables many years ago. Their keen sense of smell and hearing and their great agility made them right for that work. The original purposes are still inbred. I remember one day when one of our dogs treed a marmot and spent the whole afternoon patiently and silently sitting it out, watching the furry clump glued to a low branch. She had to be brought bodily into the house rather than give up! Others have spent hours stalking turtles or bugs.

Two Miniature Schnauzers will figuratively elbow each other and get into more mischief than one will, and several instinctively work as a pack to hold at bay any kind of intruder.

A Miniature Schnauzer is a most adaptable fellow. He can live in a house and run in a big fenced yard, or he can live in an apartment and be exercised on a leash agreeably.

A Miniature Schnauzer will put up with a certain amount of indignity if it pleases his people. Such was the case with one of our males who was the special delight of our three-year-old several years ago. At the time, she had a "thing" about colds and runny noses, and she would try to dry the dog's nose with a tissue every time he would settle down for a nap. His reaction was only a look of utter and absolute disbelief!

While some dogs are lap-cuddlers, others find this beneath their dignity and prefer being close rather than *on*. In either case, the Miniature Schnauzer will never let his humans out of his sight when it is possible to keep them in view.

Because they respond so well to human affection, even older Miniature Schnauzers can be placed in new homes happily and with relatively few adjustment problems. Miniatures also live agreeably with other pets. Surely a dominance pattern will establish itself, for this is part of Nature's laws, but if each pet is given the attention he needs, such social relationships can be compatible. Our neighbor once had a pet rabbit which hopped freely in its back yard much of the time. This situation was the bane of our existence until we decided that the animals would have to work out their own problems. As it turned out, our dogs and the rabbit became great playmates, with each running along his side of the fence trying to outdo the other. Much as I hate to admit it, I think the rabbit frequently outsmarted the dogs—he'd turn on a dime and hide behind a tree, leaving the bewildered Schnauzers sniffing and searching for this "thing" which apparently had vanished into thin air. About the time the dogs would concede the loss, the rabbit would pop out from his hiding place and the game would start again.

Most Miniature Schnauzers perform exceptionally well in obedience work. Of course, if the dog doesn't want to do his "downs" in wet, cold grass (as was the dilemma of one of our friends), I personally can't condemn him! While trainable, most Miniature Schnauzers are not usually natural retrievers. Many Miniature Schnauzers succeed in acquiring titles in both conformation and obedience. Ch. Mein Herr Schnapps, U.D., was the first Miniature Schnauzer in history to attain dual titles—in his case, simultaneously. His owner tells that perhaps one of the things that was most remarkable about him was the fact that he immediately recognized a change in collar (from conformation to obedience). She remembers running between the two rings at the shows, and how he unfailingly knew how to stand and pose in the show ring and equally fast how to sit in the obedience ring. Unaffected by her honor, a top obedience Terrier in the country, Miniature Schnauzer Dardane Nocturne, is a family pet; and many champions spend non-showing days behaving just like regular dogs.

On occasion, Miniature Schnauzers have been in promotional ads and films. One such movie was the 1955 production, *The Bar Sinister,* in which several Miniature Schnauzers of the Elfland Kennels appeared. Two champions, Adam, U.D., and Annabelle, and a young dog named Eric performed. The latter, his owner relates, really seemed to enjoy the bright lights, heat, and confusion, and turned out to be a real ham.

One animal-behavior authority feels that those of us who own bewhiskered breeds miss a great deal of pleasure because many of the dog's facial expressions are hidden beneath the beard and brows. While I admit to being totally prejudiced, I disagree entirely, having noted emotions ranging from sheer pleasure to pain and from inquisitiveness to concentration, expressions of sympathy, anger, teasing, concern, trust, and more—all clearly exhibited. And I do think that the Miniature Schnauzer does have a sense of humor. As an example, one of our dogs continually throws his favorite ball under the sofa and then stares penetratingly at it and at me until I must stop whatever I'm doing to retrieve his ball. And from his expression when he succeeds in cajoling me into doing as he wishes, I'm convinced that he's laughing at me!

Barinet Cha Cha Cha, American UD, Canadian CD.

The Miniature Schnauzer in the Obedience Ring

Obedience training, either to improve household manners or to compete in A.K.C. trials, is another rewarding area open to Miniature Schnauzer enthusiasts. In this venture our breed fares very well.

Each month the "Gazette," official monthly publication of the A.K.C., includes the name of each dog awarded a championship title or an obedience degree. The list of Miniature Schnauzers that have earned a Companion Dog or higher degree is growing impressively longer each year. In the ten year period between 1936 (when official A.K.C. obedience trial rules were set) and 1946, only fourteen C.D. and two C.D.X. degrees were acquired by Miniature Schnauzers. There clearly was not much interest in obedience training then—and, in addition, Miniature Schnauzer registrations were low at that time. Currently, registrations are high, and there is great interest in both dog training and breed competition. In 1971 alone, the total awards for Miniature Schnauzers, according to "Gazette" reports, were as follows: 112 bench champions, 140 Companion Dogs, twenty-nine Companion Dogs Excellent, ten Utility Dogs, and one Tracking Dog. Of these obedience-trained dogs, ten had previously won their championships. It is obvious that Schnauzers are not just pretty faces and fluffy legs, but creatures of high intelligence, too.

Before 1936 there were no official A.K.C. rules for obedience trials, although a few unofficial obedience classes were held at some shows. It was in such classes that Ch. Mussolini of Marienhof completed his C.D. requirements with high placements. However, scores in these classes were never recognized by the A.K.C., so the credit as the first officially recorded Miniature Schnauzer to be awarded an obedience degree goes to Mrs. Marian Shaw's dog, Shaw's Little Pepper, who later acquired the title of "champion" before his name.

In 1949, Playboy of Kenhoff became the first Miniature Schnauzer to complete requirements for the ultimate, the U.D.T. The same year, Brunhilde v. Stortsborg became the first bitch to earn a U.D. Fred v. Schonhardt of Crystal was the first black to win a C.D.

Every dog is an individual, and it is a wise handler who knows and understands his dog's personality and learns to train him accordingly. Most Miniature Schnauzers do not require a heavy hand; they respond most effectively to a firm tone of voice and usually are happy to please. However, they are independent—a quality which can be frustrating; but this independence gives them much ability to think for themselves. Watch a Schnauzer concentrating on scent discrimination and you know he's thinking. And surely intelligence varies, for genetics count in this respect, too. Nevertheless, there is nothing so unattractive as a broken-spirited dog of any breed in the ring, even though he may perform his tasks to the letter; so the moral of the story is that training, done correctly, can be fun for both the canine and the human.

Mrs. Lois Ready, owner and trainer of Lady Gretchen Frost, C.D.X., Mexican P.C., tells how Gretchen hated the breed ring beyond words and never put her tail or ears up when being shown in conformation. However, in obedience she was completely the opposite and sparkled with delight. She loved to jump and to retrieve, and the bigger the audience, the better! Her untimely death cut short a potentially promising record.

Most authorities agree that obedience lessons are best learned in classes with other dogs and their handlers, so that the dog will become accustomed to a social and business atmosphere. In many areas of the country, the local humane societies offer basic training classes. There are also ever-growing numbers of dog training clubs, and even more specifically, many Miniature Schnauzer clubs offer courses in both obedience and conformation training for their members.

A large majority of experienced trainers feel that it is best to approach the championship and obedience degree quests separately so that there will be less confusion to the dog, particularly regarding sitting and gaiting. Mrs. Laura Getz's Ch. Mein Herr Schnapps, U.D., the first Miniature Schnauzer in history to acquire this combination of awards, seems to be an exception. This 1955 Highest Scoring Terrier in the nation, once won the Terrier Group and Highest Scoring Dog in Trial on the same day! Schnapps also had an avid love of water and retrieved live ducks like a pro!

Most authorities will agree that training should be started at as early an age as possible. Puppy kindergarten classes are offered for the young ones so that they can learn to sit, lie down, come when called, and walk politely on a leash, as well as to be quiet, to be housebroken, and to be pretty much under control—in other words, nice to have around a home—by the time they are eight to twenty-eight weeks of age.

Obedience training for A.K.C. trials appeals to many fanciers because the competition is fundamentally against one's self. In the breed

Ch. Mein Herr Schnapps, UD, clears a jump.

Barinet Cha Cha Cha, American UD, Canadian CD

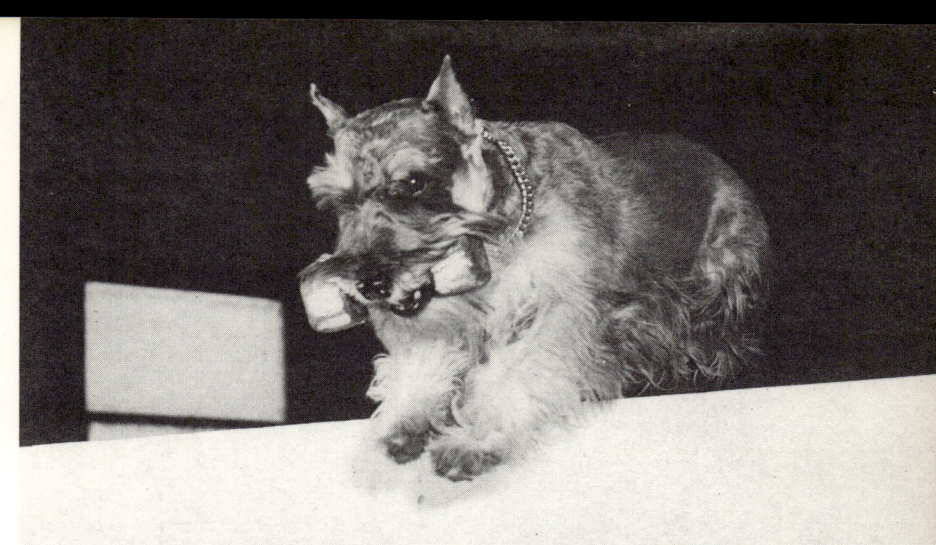

ring, there can be only one winner from perhaps many worthy specimens; in obedience, any deserving dog will qualify. Dogs that are spayed, clipped, or possess disqualifying features may compete in obedience, for they are not judged on conformation.

Many fine publications are available to aid those interested in obedience. Two books most helpful in offering training techniques (though differing in approach) are *Training You to Train Your Dog,* by Blanche Saunders, and *Dog Obedience Training,* by Milo Pearsall.

Obedience trained dogs (or the equivalent), especially those of good quality, those kept in top coat condition, and those whose expressions project engaging personalities, are sought after by animal talent agencies for films, commercials, live stage work, modeling, and promotions. Mrs. Gloria Lewis' lovely Ch. Blythewood Her Highness, C.D., and her nursing babies were guests on the Captain Kangaroo T.V. program in 1970, and evidenced every possible manifestation of desirable conformation and perfect temperament and grooming.

In addition to Mrs. Florence Bradburn's Elfland Miniature Schnauzers that took part in the 1955 filming of *The Bar Sinister,* by Richard Harding Davis, Hamann's Adolph the Awful, C.D., was in a Purina Dog Food documentary film in 1962.

Top obedience Miniature Schnauzers have been a tremendous credit to the breed. Canadian and American Ch. Jonaire Pocono Rough Rider, Canadian and American U.D.T. (owned and handled by Dr. R. J. H. Stanton), lived to slightly over fifteen years of age and reigned as the only champion U.D.T. in the breed. He was the first dog of any breed to achieve all of these titles—the U.D.T. in 1958 and the bench title in 1959. He scored numerous perfect scores in both American and Canadian trials and represented the Terrier Group in an obedience demonstration held at the Westminster Kennel Club Show in the late fifties.

Sambo of Cobb (1954-1967) was the first black and silver dog to earn a U.D.T. His owner, Charles Cobb, described him as a happy dog of proper size, enjoying every minute of playing to an audience, and not infrequently being an outright ham and a clown.

Hamann's Falla, U.D., was the breed's only black titlist until 1970 when a black bitch, Klien Schwarz Madchen, U.D., joined in the honor. Wyncliff Sham-O-Sari, owned by Winnie Bigelow, is believed to be the first black and silver bitch in the United States to hold the U.D. title. In addition she has a Canadian C.D.X. Mrs. Nan Ackerman's Ch. Rik-Rak Regina, C.D., of the early sixties, is the breed's only third-generation obedience-titled champion bitch. Another multi-

Sambo of Cobb, UDT

American and Canadian Ch. Jonaire Pocono Rough Rider, Canadian and American UDT

Am., Can. Ch. Marwyck Gun-Fire, CDX

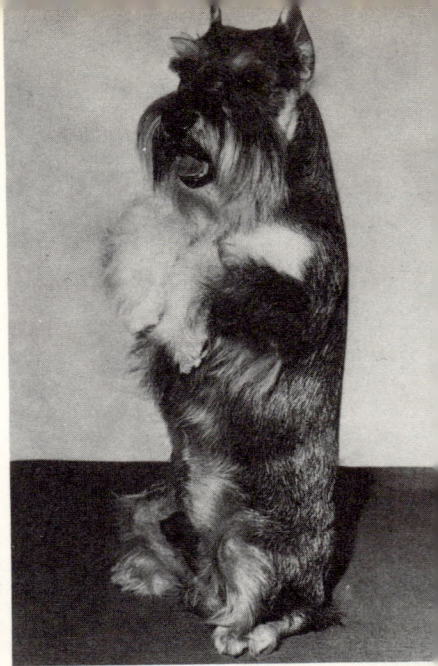

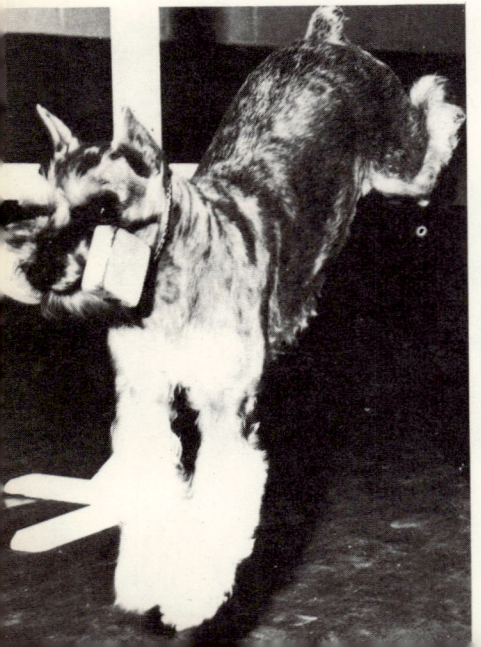

Dardane Nocturne, UD

titled dog is American and Canadian Ch. Wildwood's Showboat, Bermuda C.D., American and Canadian C.D.X., owned by Paul Miley.

In 1968, the Number One obedience Miniature Schnauzer and Terrier in the United States was Barinet Cha Cha Cha, American U.D., Canadian C.D., owned by Jeanette and Allen Stark. An all-breed record was established that year, when, in addition to Cha Cha Cha's record, Ch. Barclay Square Be Grand (also owned by the Starks) led all Miniature Schnauzers in the breed ring according to the Knight System.

1969 Group placements in obedience found the Terrier Group dominated by the breed. Of the top ten, six were Miniature Schnauzers.

Having been Number Two in 1970, Dardane Nocturne, U.D., a bitch owned and trained by Mrs. Karen Jackson, was the 1971 Number One obedience Terrier in the country.

At the 1971 National Utility Dog Tournament (competition held annually in St. Louis, Missouri), forty-seven cream-of-the-crop Utility-titled dogs representing many breeds and many states competed. While the Minis didn't make the first four placements, Dardane Nocturne tied for fifth place just one-half point behind the fourth-place winner, and Tucker Greyfrier, U.D., captured sixth place! It is interesting to note that "Gidget" (as Nocturne is known to her friends), at three years of age, was one of the youngest bitches there, and Tucker Greyfrier, at nine years of age, was one of the oldest. Tucker, trained exclusively by Mrs. Mary Lou Bowen, had been one of the top five United States obedience Miniature Schnauzers for the previous five years.

So, once again, without making a complete list, many important obedience dogs are bound to be omitted, but this overview proves that Miniature Schnauzers have demonstrated their steadiness and complete versatility, and have distinguished themselves with both beauty and brains.

I hope you enjoy the breed as much as we do, especially the greatest Miniature Schnauzer of them all—YOURS!

Am., Can. Ch. Wildwood's Showboat, Am., Can. CDX

Ch. Annabelle of Elfland as a puppy. (Photo by owner.)

Pillars of the Breed

To highlight outstanding dogs, strains, and kennels is to risk omitting worthy names, for the worthy names are numerous and their impact on the breed over the past fifty years is tremendous. The duration of time that breeders are active varies, so it must be concluded that names which belong on the list are those which demand special attention through a combination of steadfastness and outstanding show and producing records. The great ones, not discounting a little bit of luck, are born and made, and they endure! Still, the ever-growing list is all too long to capsulate in this limited space.

Most unique, of course, is Mrs. Slattery, who not only imported the dogs which began the breed in the United States, but also holds a number of firsts for the breed, is still actively breeding and exhibiting, and surely must have produced a hundred champions. Her Ch. Moses Taylor was the first American-bred champion; Ch. Mussolini of Marienhof was the first Miniature Schnauzer shown in obedience in America (1935); and Ch. Aennchen of Marienhof (owned by Mardale Kennels) was the first American-bred bitch to win a Group. Two of Marienhof's early major links in the chain which established the breed following the first imports, were Ch. Marko of Marienhof and his son Ch. T. M. G. of Marienhof, who sired thirteen and twenty champions respectively—each carrying on the line, as is evidenced in top pedigrees.

Mr. Kerns' Wollaton Kennels, Brookmeade, the kennel of Mrs. Dodge Sloan (whose import, Lenchen v. Dornbusch, was the first Miniature Schnauzer to complete an American championship), Mrs. Jeanes' Mardale Kennels, Minquas, Sharvogue, and Anfiger—all helped to settle the Miniature Schnauzer firmly in America during the breed's first years here.

Some kennels begun in the second quarter of the 1900s and active today are Ledahof, under the leadership of Mrs. Leda Martin; world-famous Handful, owned by Miss Gene Simmonds; and Dorem, established by Miss Dorothy Williams, whose lines produced consistent winners from a carefully line-bred pattern. The Dorem prefix is prominent in most winning pedigrees, with Ch. Dorem Display, whelped in 1945, the cornerstone of many kennels since. During his show career, Display was owned by Mr. and Mrs. Phil Meldon, well-known

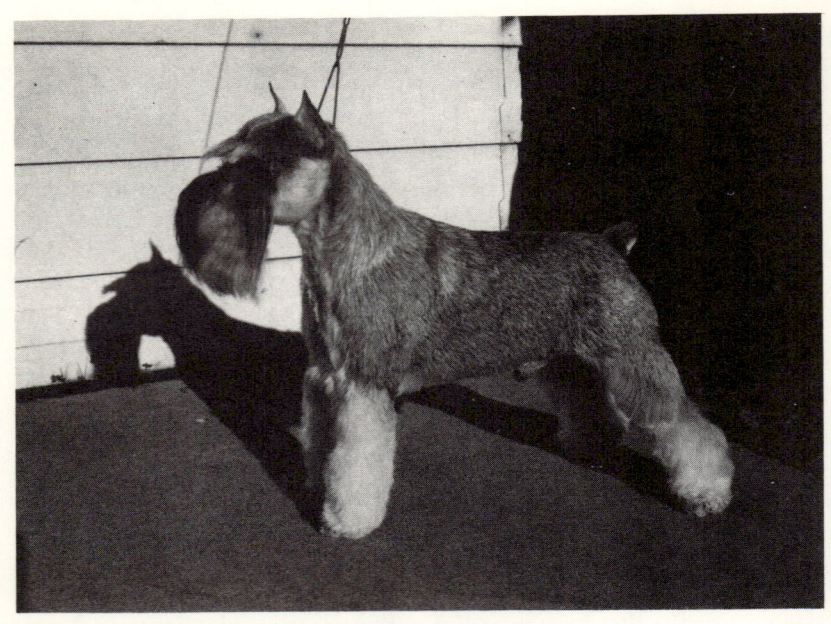

Ch. Marcheim Poppin' Fresh, Group and Specialty Winner.

Ch. Patricia of Marienhof. Photo by William Gilbert.

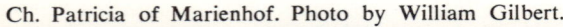

for their winning Miniature Schnauzers. In 1952, he was sold to Benrook Kennels. He was considered the Standard personified and tallied an overall show record that included five all-breed Bests in Show, four Specialty Bests, and a Group First at Westminster. He sired a total of forty-two champions, with one of his champion sons, Ch. Dorem Tribute, siring forty-one more. Another top son, Ch. Diplomat of Ledahof, sired twenty-nine more; and twice Best-in-Show winner, Ch. Meldon's Ruffian, sired another twenty-six. Imagine the influence of these few dogs alone in a network of lines.

Great dogs and their kennels become synonymous. To mention just a few of them is a problem, for more and more dogs are becoming great and breaking new records! However, just breaking records, while undoubtedly significant because of vast influence, is not the only zenith in gauging a dog's value because some dogs are not campaigned continually, and, in addition, time is required for full realization of a producer in establishing his type. In establishing type, one thinks of several generations in terms of strain type, breed type, and individual type. Frequently, after having seen a number of representatives of specific kennels, one can begin to guess kennel lines quite accurately because of certain traits manifested by particular lines.

Ch. Delfin Janus (1952-1968), a Diplomat of Ledahof son and a favorite house companion of his breeder and owner, Mrs. Mae Dickenson, was not campaigned after his twenty-fifth Best of Breed, but he left an indisputable and lasting mark as a producer, leaving thirty-seven champion offspring. I last saw Janus when he was fifteen; he was every inch the gentleman and as alert as could be. Though now inactive in breeding, the Delfin line is strongly represented in kennels all over the United States, Canada, and Great Britain.

Marwyck, Mrs. Marion Evashwick's prefix—and the inimitable American, Canadian, and Mexican Ch. Marwyck Pitt-Penn Pirate (1954-1965), a Diplomat of Ledahof grandson! This Best-in-Show winner, owned by Mr. and Mrs. Glen Fancy, is the all-time top producer with forty-seven champion-of-record get. Like father, like son—American, Canadian, and Mexican Ch. Fancway's Pirate Jr. of LaMay, owned by Mr. and Mrs. Charles Post, already claims twenty-eight champions with more on the way.

Another all-time great, Ch. Phil-Mar Lugar (1956-1970), with two Bests in Show and twenty-five champions to his credit, was just one of the many exceptional and distinctive Miniature Schnauzers produced at Phil-Mar Kennels. As a producer, his name is also known in Canada, Bermuda, Mexico, England, and Italy.

Ch. Delfin Janus at 10½ years of age.

Ch. Frevohly's Best Bon-Bon, UD, finished her championship in 1955 and her UD in 1956 and 1957.

Ch. Dardane Priam, CD

Ch. Jonaire Pocono Rock n' Roll, a top producing sire.

Best-in-Show winner Ch. Barclay Square Be Grand, Number One Miniature Schnauzer in United States in 1968 (Knight System).

Ch. Mutiny Uproar, a top winning dog, 1970.

Ch. Delfin Victoria, dam of six champions. 1955.

Ch. Blythewood Sprig of Holly, dam of three champions.

Ch. Blythewood Main Gazebo, bred and owned by Mrs. Joan Huber, is a Lugar son that currently has twenty-six champion offspring and more hopefuls preparing for the ring. Always outstanding showmen, the beautiful Blythewood Schnauzers are a controlled combination of top bloodlines resulting in a recognizable strain currently influencing the breed from coast to coast.

As with most prominent kennels which produce consistent quality, the Miniature Schnauzers of the Windy Hill Kennels of Mrs. Thelma Gould on the West Coast also represent interrelationships of top bloodlines. American, Canadian, and Mexican Ch. Windy Hill Defiance emerges as a dynamo of strong breed type.

In reflection, Mrs. Gould notes that when she bought her first Miniature Schnauzer shortly after World War II, the breed was still relatively new to the United States, and little written information was available about the breed in general, and the "care-of" in particular. Consequently, dog shows were the school grounds where one learned from other fanciers. Public awareness has become a prime consideration of breed clubs in the past few years, for not everyone can have or wants to have a top show dog or a top producer, but the average owner can certainly be informed about the breed and learn to care for his Miniature Schnauzer properly.

Any animal used for breeding is only as good as his ability to produce his own good qualities. Ch. Yankee Pride Colonel Stump (with fifteen champions to his credit), Ch. Tweed Packet of Wilkern (with fifteen champions in a too-short five-year producing span), American and Brazilian Ch. Helarry's Dark Victory (with thirty-two champions), Ch. Sandman of Sharvogue (a keystone in top pedigrees), Jonaire Kennel's long list of titled dogs with a line based on the great Ch. Benrook Buckaroo, Geelong, Abingdon, Elfland, Mutiny, Sparks, Landmark, Fancway, Arador, Barclay Square—dogs, kennels, and people become a potpourri of pillars in breed development and achievement influencing tomorrow's youngsters.

While multi-winning dogs, because of logistics, are usually campaigned by professional handlers, it is interesting to note that many titled dogs are owner conditioned and handled. In the fifties, Dick Matheny piloted his home-bred Ch. Fancyfree Fancy Package to a total of 101 Bests of Breed. The titled Travelmor Miniature Schnauzers of Mr. and Mrs. William Moore are good examples of the "do-it-yourselfers" who succeed. The Moore's distinctly "Travelmor" dog, Ch. Travelmor's Witchcraft, in particular, has earned sixty-four Bests of Breed in six years of limited showing.

Ch. Adford's Bob White

Ch. Abingdon Authority, winner of nine all-breed Bests in Show.

Am., Can., Mex. Ch. Windy Hill Defiance.

Am., Can., Mex. Ch. Marwyck Pitt-Penn Pirate.

Also, many of the owners who handled their own dogs have expanded their talents and have gone on to become the professional handlers and/or judges of today.

The males' outstanding records are indeed impressive, but the bitches' records have not yet been mentioned, and while a bitch cannot possibly compete in rank with a dog's expanse of record statistics, her importance should never be underestimated for a minute. A puppy receives his inheritance from both his sire and his dam, and where the stud's responsibility ends, the bitch's begins!

It would be safe to say that with few exceptions, top kennels were founded on their bitches. Certainly, Ch. Blythewood Merry Melody, who produced eight champions, and her daughter Ch. Blythewood Sweet Talk, dam of seven champions, are of great credit to Blythewood. Notable, too, is the fact that most of the early winners in ring competition were bitches, and over the years, several bitches have numbered among the Best-in-Show winners: Champions Penlan Parady, Miown Exotic Poppy, Winsomor Miss Kitty, Alpine Baby Ruth, Carleen Comic Caper, Wynmore Summer Song, Mutiny Pandemonium, and Phil-Mar Lucy Lady, to name a few.

Ch. Lotte v.d. Goldbachhohe, Amsel's daughter, and American and Canadian Ch. Sorceress of Ledahof, whelped in 1947 and owned by Mrs. Evashwick, tie as top-producing bitches, with a record twelve A.K.C. champions each. In addition, Sorceress has one Canadian champion. Now, about twenty-five years later, Ch. Barclay Square Becky Sharp, with eleven champions, may break another record.

Ch. Enchantress, whelped in 1944, owned by Ledahof Kennels, must be considered as one who has left an enormous influence on the breed through her outstanding offspring. In four litters, she produced eight champions, one of which was the aforementioned Ch. Diplomat of Ledahof. Ch. Gladdings Bie Bie produced ten champions and Ch. Benrook Bona produced nine. Wild Honey of Sharvogue, while not a champion herself, produced eight champions in only two litters, both of which were sired by Ch. T. M. G. of Marienhof.

To date, Ch. Frevohly's Best Bon-Bon, U.D., owned by Mrs. Ruth Zeigler, is the only bitch in the breed to hold both the championship and U.D. titles. In addition, she produced five champions.

Mrs. Fran Cazier's Orbit Miniature Schnauzers, especially the bitches, have compiled a remarkable record without extensive or excessive breeding—emphasizing again that it is quality, not quantity, that really counts. Orbit's matron, Minchette Maier, produced six champions.

Lists of top producers with the number of their champion get are published annually in "Schnauzer Shorts," a monthly magazine about Schnauzers. October is the special stud issue and July features the bitches.

Recognition must also be given the colors other than salt and pepper. Today, salt and pepper is consistently the most popular color, so it is natural that top Miniature Schnauzers would be salt and pepper. However, currently, an upswing in interest in the blacks and the black and silvers has brought forward noteworthy specimens in those colors.

Many of the early imported and American-bred Miniature Schnauzers were black, so many present blacks trace back to the same top lines as do the salt and peppers. Because of this and because of the fact that salt and pepper crosses are legal in this country, it is impossible to name major producing lines of solid blacks.

The first solid black champion was Cunning of Asta (1935-1951), who won the title in 1936. She was bred by Mrs. Willia Maguire, whose interest in blacks dates back to 1933. Recently, a black bitch, Ch. Johnson's Ebony Kwicksilver, finished to become the first American-bred black to attain the championship title in the United States in over twenty-five years, and now Woodhaven Black Cough Drops has become the first American-bred black male to accomplish the same feat.

Can., Am. Ch. Sylva Sprite Snowy Mittens, whelped 1969. Top Canadian-bred Schnauzer for 1970 (black and silver).

Those interested in blacks will find camaraderie in The Black Miniature Schnauzer Fanciers Association, a club with a self-explanatory name!

Unlike the dominant black genes, the black and silver genes are recessive. In oversimplified terms, this means that BOTH parents must carry the black and silver genes in order to produce black and silver puppies. Therefore, black and silver can result from salt and pepper parents. Sometimes puppies thought to be black and silver in their early months, mature into very dark salt and peppers. In 1938, Inka of Aspen Hill won the first coveted title for a black and silver. Today there are many fine black and silver breeders—Tigerland, Dorovan, Walsh, Hendricks, and Silva Sprite (in Canada), to name a few, are making their mark.

In 1970, the American Miniature Schnauzer Club voted to offer separate classes for blacks and black and silvers at all of its specialty shows. This gives these minority individuals a much better chance for the recognition they deserve within the breed.

So, be it business or pleasure, records or not, we've gone to the dogs!

Minchette Maier (photo by owner—1964). Dam of six AKC champions from total of fifteen puppies whelped. Whelped 1959, on West Coast since 1964.

Ch. Blythewood Ricochet of LaMay, sire of fifteen champions.

Winners at American Miniature Schnauzer Club Specialty, New York, February 10, 1963. Judge, Dorothy Williams. Left to right: RWD, Luvemal's Upper Crust (handled by C. Stacy); WD, Top Notch Crescendo (handled by J. Hardie); BOS, Ch. Yankee Squadron Leader (handled by E. Dobbins); BB and WB, Geelong Enchanting Miss (handled by W. Moore); RWB, Glenshaw's Ginger Peachy (handled by Mrs. Snowden).

Manners for the Family Dog

Although each dog has personality quirks and idiosyncrasies that set him apart as an individual, dogs in general have two characteristics that can be utilized to advantage in training. The first is the dog's strong desire to please, which has been built up through centuries of association with man. The second lies in the innate quality of the dog's mentality. It has been proved conclusively that while dogs have reasoning power, their learning ability is based on a direct association of cause and effect, so that they willingly repeat acts that bring pleasant results and discontinue acts that bring unpleasant results. Hence, to take fullest advantage of a dog's abilities, the trainer must make sure the dog understands a command, and then reward him when he obeys and correct him when he does wrong.

Commands should be as short as possible and should be repeated in the same way, day after day. Saying "Heel," one day, and "Come here and heel," the next will confuse the dog. *Heel, sit, stand, stay, down,* and *come* are standard terminology, and are preferable for a dog that may later be given advanced training.

Tone of voice is important, too. For instance, a coaxing tone helps cajole a young puppy into trying something new. Once an exercise is mastered, commands given in a firm, matter-of-fact voice give the dog confidence in his own ability. Praise, expressed in an exuberant tone will tell the dog quite clearly that he has earned his master's approval. On the other hand, a firm "No" indicates with equal clarity that he has done wrong.

Rewards for good performance may consist simply of praising lavishly and petting the dog, although many professional trainers use bits of food as rewards. Tidbits are effective only if the dog is hungry, of course. And if you smoke, you must be sure to wash your hands before each training session, for the odor of nicotine is repulsive to dogs. On the hands of a heavy smoker, the odor of nicotine may be so strong that the dog is unable to smell the tidbit.

Correction for wrong-doing should be limited to repeating "No," in a scolding tone of voice or to confining the dog to his bed. Spanking or striking the dog is taboo—particularly using sticks, which might cause injury, but the hand should never be used either. For field training as well as some obedience work, the hand is used to signal the dog. Dogs that have been punished by slapping have a tendency to cringe whenever they see a hand raised and consequently do not respond promptly when the owner's intent is not to punish but to signal.

Some trainers recommend correcting the dog by whacking him with a rolled-up newspaper. The idea is that the newspaper will not injure the dog but that the resulting noise will condition the dog to avoid repeating the act that seemingly caused the noise. Many authorities object to this type of correction, for it may result in the dog's becoming "noise-shy"—a decided disadvantage with show dogs which must maintain poise in adverse, often noisy, situations. "Noise-shyness" is also an unfortunate reaction in field dogs, since it may lead to gun-shyness.

To be effective, correction must be administered immediately, so that in the dog's mind there is a direct connection between his act and the correction. You can make voice corrections under almost any circumstances, but you must never call the dog to you and then correct him, or he will associate the correction with the fact that he has come and will become reluctant to respond. If the dog is at a distance and doing something he shouldn't, go to him and scold him while he is still involved in wrong-doing. If this is impossible, ignore the offense until he repeats it and you can correct him properly.

Especially while a dog is young, he should be watched closely and stopped before he gets into mischief. All dogs need to do a certain amount of chewing, so to prevent your puppy's chewing something you value, provide him with his own rubber balls and toys. Never allow him to chew cast-off slippers and then expect him to differentiate between cast-off items and those you value. Nylon stockings, wooden articles, and various other items may cause intestinal obstructions if the dog chews and swallows them, and death may result. So it is essential that the dog be permitted to chew only on bones or rubber toys.

Serious training for obedience should not be started until a dog is a year old. But basic training in house manners should begin the day the puppy enters his new home. A puppy should never be given the run of the house but should be confined to a box or small pen except for play periods when you can devote full attention to him. The first thing to teach the dog is his name, so that whenever he hears it, he will immediately come to attention. Whenever you are near his box, talk to him, using his name repeatedly. During play periods, talk to him, pet him, and handle him, for he must be conditioned so he will not object to being handled by a veterinarian, show judge, or family friend. As the dog investigates his surroundings, watch him carefully and if he tries something he shouldn't, reprimand him with a scolding "No!" If he repeats the offense, scold him and confine him to his box, then praise him. Discipline must be prompt, consistent, and always followed with praise. Never tease the dog, and never allow others to do so. Kindness and understanding are essential to a pleasant, mutually rewarding relationship.

When the puppy is two to three months old, secure a flat, narrow leather collar and have him start wearing it (never use a harness, which will encourage tugging and pulling). After a week or so, attach a light leather lead to the collar during play sessions and let the puppy walk around, dragging the lead behind him. Then start holding the end of the lead and coaxing the puppy to come to you. He will then be fully accustomed to collar and lead when you start taking him outside while he is being housebroken.

Housebreaking can be accomplished in a matter of approximately two weeks provided you wait until the dog is mature enough to have some control over bodily functions. This is usually at about four months. Until that time, the puppy should spend most of his day confined to his penned area, with the floor covered with several thicknesses of newspapers so that he may relieve himself when necessary without damage to floors.

Either of two methods works well in housebreaking—the choice depending upon where you live. If you live in a house with a readily accessible yard, you will probably want to train the puppy from the beginning to go outdoors. If you live in an apartment without easy access to a yard, you may decide to train him first to relieve himself on newspapers and then when he has learned control, to teach the puppy to go outdoors.

If you decide to train the puppy by taking him outdoors, arrange some means of confining him indoors where you can watch him closely—in a small penned area, or tied to a short lead (five or six feet). Dogs are naturally clean animals, reluctant to soil their quarters, and confining the puppy to a limited area will encourage him to avoid making a mess.

A young puppy must be taken out often, so watch your puppy closely and if he indicates he is about to relieve himself, take him out at once. If he has an accident, scold him and take him out so he will associate the act of going outside with the need to relieve himself. Always take the puppy out within an hour after meals—preferably to the same place each time—and make sure he relieves himself before you return him to the house. Restrict his water for two hours before bedtime and take him out just before you retire for the night. Then, as soon as you wake in the morning, take him out again.

For paper training, set aside a particular room and cover a large area of the floor with several thicknesses of newspapers. Confine the dog on a short leash and each time he relieves himself, remove the soiled papers and replace them with clean ones.

As his control increases, gradually decrease the paper area, leaving part of the floor bare. If he uses the bare floor, scold him mildly and put him on the papers, letting him know that there is where he is to relieve himself. As he comes to understand the idea, increase the bare area until papers cover only space equal to approximately two full newspaper sheets. Keep him using the papers, but begin taking him on a leash to the street at the times of day that he habitually relieves himself. Watch him closely when he is indoors and at the first sign that he needs to go, take him outdoors. Restrict his water for two hours before bedtime, but if necessary, permit him to use the papers before you retire for the night.

Using either method, the puppy will be housebroken in an amazingly short time. Once he has learned control he will need to relieve himself only four or five times a day.

Informal obedience training, started at the age of about six to eight months, will provide a good background for any advanced training you may decide to give your dog later. The collar most

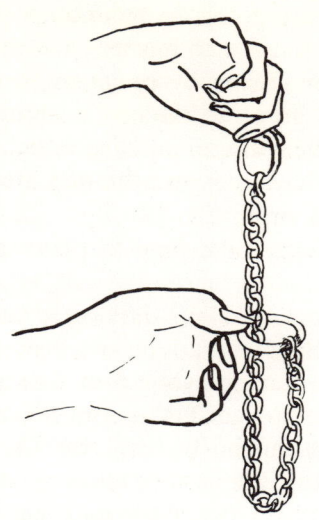 

effective for training is the metal chain-link variety. The correct size for your dog will be about one inch longer than the measurement around the largest part of his head. The chain must be slipped through one of the rings so the collar forms a loop. The collar should be put on with the loose ring at the right of the dog's neck, the chain attached to it coming over the neck and through the holding ring, rather than under the neck. Since the dog is to be at your left during most of the training, this makes the collar most effective.

The leash should be attached to the loose ring, and should be either webbing or leather, six feet long and a half inch to a full inch wide. When you want your dog's attention, or wish to correct him, give a light, quick pull on the leash, which will momentarily tighten the collar about the neck. Release the pressure instantly, and the correction will have been made. If the puppy is already accustomed to a leather collar, he will adjust easily to the training collar. But before you start training sessions, practice walking with the dog until he responds readily when you increase tension on the leash.

Set aside a period of fifteen minutes, once or twice a day, for regular training sessions, and train in a place where there will be no distractions. Teach only one exercise at a time, making sure the dog has mastered it before going on to another. It will probably take at least a week for the dog to master each exercise. As training progresses, start each session by reviewing exercises the dog has already learned, then go on to the new exercise for a period of concerted practice. When discipline is required, make the correction immediately, and always praise the dog after corrections as well as when he obeys promptly. During each session stick strictly to business. Afterwards, take time to play with the dog.

The first exercise to teach is heeling. Have the dog at your left and hold the leash as shown in the illustration on the preceding page. Start walking, and just as you put your foot forward for the first step, say your dog's name to get his attention, followed by the command, "Heel!" Simultaneously, pull on the leash lightly. As you walk, try to keep the dog at your left side, with his head alongside your left leg. Pull on the leash as necessary to urge him forward or back, to right or left, but keep him in position. Each time you pull on the leash, say "Heel!" and praise the dog lavishly. When the dog heels properly in a straight line, start making circles, turning corners, etc.

Once the dog has learned to heel well, start teaching the "sit." Each time you stop while heeling, command "Sit!" The dog will be at your left, so use your left hand to press on his rear and guide him to a sitting position, while you use the leash in your right hand to keep his head up. Hold him in position for a few moments while you praise him, then give the command to heel. Walk a few steps, stop, and repeat the procedure. Before long he will automatically sit whenever you stop. You can then teach the dog to "sit" from any position.

When the dog will sit on command without correction, he is ready to learn to stay until you release him. Simply sit him, command "Stay!" and hold him in position for perhaps half a minute, repeating "Stay," if he attempts to stand. You can release him by saying "O.K." Gradually increase the time until he will stay on command for three or four minutes.

The "stand-stay" should also be taught when the dog is on leash. While you are heeling, stop and give the command "Stand!" Keep the dog from sitting by quickly placing your left arm under him, immediately in front of his right hind leg. If he continues to try to sit, don't scold him but start up again with the heel command, walk a few steps, and stop again, repeating the stand command and preventing the dog from sitting. Once the dog has mastered the stand, teach him to stay by holding him in position and repeating the word "Stay!"

The "down stay" will prove beneficial in many situations, but especially if you wish to take your dog in the car without confining him to a crate. To teach the "down," have the dog sitting at your side with collar and leash on. If he is a large dog, step forward with the leash in your hand and turn so you face him. Let the leash touch the floor, then step over it with your right foot so it is under the instep of your shoe. Grasping the leash low down with both hands, slowly pull up, saying, "Down!" Hold the leash taut until the dog goes down. Once he responds well, teach the dog to stay in the down position (the down-stay), using the same method as for the sit- and stand-stays.

To teach small dogs the "down," another method may be used. Have the dog sit at your side, then kneel beside him. Reach across his back with your left arm, and take hold of his left front leg close to the body. At the same time, with your right hand take hold of his right front leg close to his body. As you command "Down!" gently lift the legs and place the dog in the down position. Release your hold on his legs and slide your left hand onto his back, repeating, "Down, stay," while keeping him in position.

The "come" is taught when the dog is on leash and heeling. Simply walk along, then suddenly take a step backward, saying "Come!" Pull the leash as you give the command and the dog will turn and follow you. Continue walking backward, repeatedly saying "Come," and tightening the leash if necessary.

Once the dog has mastered the exercises while on leash, try taking the leash off and going through the same routine, beginning with the heeling exercise. If the dog doesn't respond promptly, he needs review with the leash on. But patience and persistence will be rewarded, for you will have a dog you can trust to respond promptly under all conditions.

Even after they are well trained, dogs sometimes develop bad habits that are hard to break. Jumping on people is a common habit, and all members of the family must assist if it is to be broken. If the dog is a large or medium breed, take a step forward and raise your knee just as he starts to jump on you. As your knee strikes the dog's chest, command "Down!" in a scolding voice. When a small dog jumps on you, take both front paws in your hands, and, while talking in a pleasant tone of voice, step on the dog's back feet just hard enough to hurt them slightly. With either method the dog is taken by surprise and doesn't associate the discomfort with the person causing it.

Occasionally a dog may be too chummy with guests who don't care for dogs. If the dog has had obedience training, simply command "Come!" When he responds, have him sit beside you.

Excessive barking is likely to bring complaints from neighbors, and persistent efforts may be needed to subdue a dog that barks without provocation. To correct the habit, you must be close to the dog when he starts barking. Encircle his muzzle with both hands, hold his mouth shut, and command "Quiet!" in a firm voice. He should soon learn to respond so you can control him simply by giving the command.

Sniffing other dogs is an annoying habit. If the dog is off leash and sniffs other dogs, ignoring your commands to come, he needs to review the lessons on basic behavior. When the dog is on leash, scold him, then pull on the leash, command "Heel," and walk away from the other dog.

A well-trained dog will be no problem if you decide to take him with you when you travel. No matter how well he responds, however, he should never be permitted off leash when you walk him in a strange area. Distractions will be more tempting, and there will be more chance of his being attacked by other dogs. So whenever the dog travels with you, take his collar and leash along—and use them.

Bench Shows

Centuries ago, it was common practice to hold agricultural fairs in conjunction with spring and fall religious festivals, and to these gatherings, cattle, dogs, and other livestock were brought for exchange. As time went on, it became customary to provide entertainment, too. Dogs often participated in such sporting events as bull baiting, bear baiting, and ratting. Then the dog that exhibited the greatest skill in the arena was also the one that brought the highest price when time came for barter or sale. Today, these fairs seem a far cry from our highly organized bench shows and field trials. But they were the forerunners of modern dog shows and played an important role in shaping the development of purebred dogs.

The first organized dog show was held at Newcastle, England, in 1859. Later that same year, a show was held at Birmingham. At both shows dogs were divided into four classes and only Pointers and Setters were entered. In 1860, the first dog show in Germany was held at Apoldo, where nearly one hundred dogs were exhibited and entries were divided into six groups. Interest expanded rapidly, and by the time the Paris Exhibition was held in 1878, the dog show was a fixture of international importance.

In the United States, the first organized bench show was held in 1874 in conjunction with the meeting of the Illinois State Sportsmen's Association in Chicago, and all entries were dogs of sporting breeds. Although the show was a rather casual affair, interest spread quickly. Before the end of the year, shows were held in Oswego, New York, Mineola, Long Island, and Memphis, Tennessee. And the latter combined a bench show with the first organized field trial ever held in the United States. In January 1875, an all-breed show (the first in the United States) was held at Detroit, Michigan. From then on, interest increased rapidly, though rules were not always uniform, for there was no organization through which to coordinate activities until September 1884

Benching area at Westminster Kennel Club Show.

Judging for Best in Show at Westminster Kennel Club Show.

when The American Kennel Club was founded. Now the largest dog registering organization in the world, the A.K.C. is an association of several hundred member clubs—all breed, specialty, field trial, and obedience groups—each represented by a delegate to the A.K.C.

The several thousand shows and trials held annually in the United States do much to stimulate interest in breeding to produce better looking, sounder, purebred dogs. For breeders, shows provide a means of measuring the merits of their work as compared with accomplishments of other breeders. For hundreds of thousands of dog fanciers, they provide an absorbing hobby.

For both spectators and participating owners, field trials constitute a fascinating demonstration of dogs competing under actual hunting conditions, where emphasis is on excellence of performance. The trials are sponsored by clubs or associations of persons interested in hunting dogs. Trials for Pointing breeds, Dachshunds, Retrievers, Spaniels, and Beagles are under the jurisdiction of The American Kennel Club and information concerning such activities is published in "Pure Bred Dogs—American Kennel Gazette." Trials for Bird Dogs are run by rules and regulations of the Amateur Field Trial Clubs of America and information concerning them is published in "The American Field."

All purebred dogs of recognized breeds may be registered with The American Kennel Club and those of hunting breeds may also be registered with The American Field. Dogs that have won championships both in the field and in bench shows are known as dual champions.

At bench (or conformation) shows, dogs are rated comparatively on their physical qualities (or conformation) in accordance with breed Standards which have been approved by The American Kennel Club. Characteristics such as size, coat, color, placement of eye or ear, general soundness, etc., are the basis for selecting the best dog in a class. Only purebred dogs are eligible to compete and if the show is one where points toward a championship are to be awarded, a dog must be at least six months old.

Bench shows are of various types. An all-breed show has classes for all of the breeds recognized by The American Kennel Club as well as a Miscellaneous Class for breeds not recognized, such as the Australian Cattle Dog, the Ibizan Hound, the Spinoni Italiani, the Tibetan Terrier, etc. A sanctioned match is an informal meeting where dogs compete but not for championship points. A specialty show is confined to a single breed. Other shows may restrict entries to champions of record, to American-bred dogs, etc. Competition for Junior Showmanship or for Best Brace, Best Team, or Best Local Dog may be included. Also, obedience competition is held in conjunction with many bench shows.

The term "bench show" is somewhat confusing in that shows of this type may be either "benched" or "unbenched." At the former, each dog is assigned an individual numbered stall where he must remain throughout the show except for times when he is being judged, groomed, or exercised. At unbenched shows, no stalls are provided and dogs are kept in their owners' cars or in crates when not being judged.

A show where a dog is judged for conformation actually constitutes an elimination contest. To begin with, the dogs of a single breed compete with others of their breed in one of the regular classes: Puppy, Novice, Bred by Exhibitor, American-Bred, or Open, and, finally, Winners, where the top dogs of the preceding five classes meet. The next step is the judging for Best of Breed (or Best of Variety of Breed). Here the Winners Dog and Winners Bitch (or the dog named Winners if only one prize is awarded) compete with any champions that are entered, together with any undefeated dogs that have competed in additional non-regular classes. The dog named Best of Breed (or Best of Variety of Breed), then goes on to compete with the other Best of Breed winners in his Group. The dogs that win in Group competition then compete for the final and highest honor, Best in Show.

When the Winners Class is divided by sex, championship points are awarded the Winners Dog and Winners Bitch. If the Winners Class is not divided by sex, championship points are awarded the dog or bitch named Winners. The number of points awarded varies, depending upon such factors as the number of dogs competing, the Schedule of Points established by the Board of Directors of the A.K.C., and whether the dog goes on to win Best of Breed, the Group, and Best in Show.

In order to become a champion, a dog must win fifteen points, including points from at least two major wins—that is, at least two shows where three or more points are awarded. The major wins must be under two different judges, and one or more of the remaining points must be won under a third judge. The most points ever awarded at a show is five and the least is one, so, in order to become

Junior Showmanship Competition at Westminster Kennel Club Show.

a champion, a dog must be exhibited and win in at least three shows, and usually he is shown many times before he wins his championship.

"Pure Bred Dogs—American Kennel Gazette" and other dog magazines contain lists of forthcoming shows, together with names and addresses of sponsoring organizations to which you may write for entry forms and information relative to fees, closing dates, etc. Before entering your dog in a show for the first time, you should familiarize yourself with the regulations and rules governing competition. You may secure such information from The American Kennel Club or from a local dog club specializing in your breed. It is essential that you also familiarize yourself with the A.K.C. approved Standard for your breed so you will be fully aware of characteristics worthy of merit as well as those considered faulty, or possibly even serious enough to disqualify the dog from competition. For instance, monorchidism (failure of one testicle to descend) and cryptorchidism (failure of both testicles to descend) are disqualifying faults in all breeds.

If possible, you should first attend a show as a spectator and observe judging procedures from ringside. It will also be helpful to join a local breed club and to participate in sanctioned matches before entering an all-breed show.

The dog should be equipped with a narrow leather show lead and a show collar—never an ornamented or spiked collar. For benched shows, a metal-link bench chain will be needed to fasten the dog to the bench. For unbenched shows, the dog's crate should be taken along so that he may be confined in comfort when he is not appearing in the ring. A dog should never be left in a car with all the windows closed. In hot weather the temperature will become unbearable in a very short time. Heat exhaustion may result from even a short period of confinement, and death may ensue.

Food and water dishes will be needed, as well as a supply of the food and water to which the dog is accustomed. Brushes and combs are also necessary, so that you may give the dog's coat a final grooming after you arrive at the show.

Familiarize yourself with the schedule of classes ahead of time, for the dog must be fed and exercised and permitted to relieve himself, and any last-minute grooming completed before his class is called. Both you and the dog should be ready to enter the ring unhurriedly. A good deal of skill in conditioning, training, and handling is required if a dog is to be presented properly. And it is essential that the handler himself be composed, for a jittery handler will transmit his nervousness to his dog.

Once the class is assembled in the ring, the judge will ask that the dogs be paraded in line, moving counter-clockwise in a circle. If you have trained your dog well, you will have no difficulty controlling him in the ring, where he must change pace quickly and gracefully and walk and trot elegantly and proudly with head erect. The show dog must also stand quietly for inspection, posing like a statue for several minutes while the judge observes his structure in detail, examines teeth, feet, coat, etc. When the judge calls your dog forward for individual inspection, do not attempt to converse, but answer any questions he may ask.

As the judge examines the class, he measures each dog against the ideal described in the Standard, then measures the dogs against each other in a comparative sense and selects for first place the dog that comes closest to conforming to the Standard for its breed. If your dog isn't among the winners, don't grumble. If he places first, don't brag loudly. For a bad loser is disgusting, but a poor winner is insufferable.

Obedience Competition

For hundreds of years, dogs have been used in England and Germany in connection with police and guard work, and their working potential has been evaluated through tests devised to show agility, strength, and courage. Organized training has also been popular with English and German breeders for many years, although it was first practiced primarily for the purpose of training large breeds in aggressive tactics.

There was little interest in obedience training in the United States until 1933 when Mrs. Whitehouse Walker returned from England and enthusiastically introduced the sport. Two years later, Mrs. Walker persuaded The American Kennel Club to approve organized obedience activities and to assume jurisdiction over obedience rules. Since then, interest has increased at a phenomenal rate, for obedience competition is not only a sport the average spectator can follow readily, but also a sport for which the average owner can train his own dog easily. Obedience competition is suitable for all breeds. Furthermore, there is no limit to the number of dogs that may win in competition, for each dog is scored individually on the basis of a point rating system.

The dog is judged on his response to certain commands, and if he gains a high enough score in three successive trials under different judges, he wins an obedience degree. Degrees awarded are "C.D."—Companion Dog; "C.D.X."—Companion Dog Excellent; and "U.D." —Utility Dog. A fourth degree, the "T.D.," or Tracking Dog degree, may be won at any time and tests for it are held apart from dog shows. The qualifying score is a minimum of 170 points out of a possible total of 200, with no score in any one exercise less than 50% of the points allotted.

Since obedience titles are progressive, earlier titles (with the exception of the tracking degree) are dropped as a dog acquires the next higher degree. If an obedience title is gained in another country in addition to the United States, that fact is signified by the word "International," followed by the title.

Trials for obedience trained dogs are held at most of the larger bench shows, and obedience training clubs are to be found in almost all communities today. Information concerning forthcoming trials and lists of obedience training clubs are included regularly in "Pure Bred Dogs—American Kennel Gazette"—and other dog magazines. Pamphlets containing rules and regulations governing obedience competition are available upon request from The American Kennel Club, 51 Madison Avenue, New York, N.Y. 10010. Rules are revised occasionally, so if you are interested in participating in obedience competition, you should be sure your copy of the regulations is current.

All dogs must comply with the same rules, although in broad jump, high jump, and bar jump competition, the jumps are adjusted to the size of the breed. Classes at obedience trials are divided into Novice (A and B), Open (A and B), and Utility (which may be divided into A and B, at the option of the sponsoring club and with the approval of The American Kennel Club).

The Novice class is for dogs that have not won the title Companion Dog. In Novice A, no person who has previously handled a dog that has won a C.D. title in the obedience ring at a licensed or member trial, and no person who has regularly trained such a dog, may enter or handle a dog. The handler must be the dog's owner or a member of the owner's immediate family. In Novice B, dogs may be handled by the owner or any other person.

The Open A class is for dogs that have won the C.D. title but have not won the C.D.X. title. Obedience judges and licensed handlers may not enter or handle dogs in this class. Each dog must be handled by the owner or by a member of his immediate family. The Open B class is for dogs that have won the title C.D. or C.D.X. A dog may continue to compete in this class after it has won the title U.D. Dogs in this class may be handled by the owner or any other person.

The Utility class is for dogs that have won the title C.D.X. Dogs that have won the title U.D. may continue to compete in this class, and dogs may be handled by the owner or any other person. Provided the A.K.C. approves, a club may choose to divide the Utility class into Utility A and Utility B. When this is done, the Utility A class is for dogs that have won the title C.D.X. and have not won the title U.D. Obedience judges and licensed handlers may not enter or handle dogs in this class. All other dogs that are eligible for the Utility class but not eligible for Utility A may be entered in Utility B.

Novice competition includes such exercises as heeling on and off lead, the stand for examination, coming on recall, and the long sit and the long down.

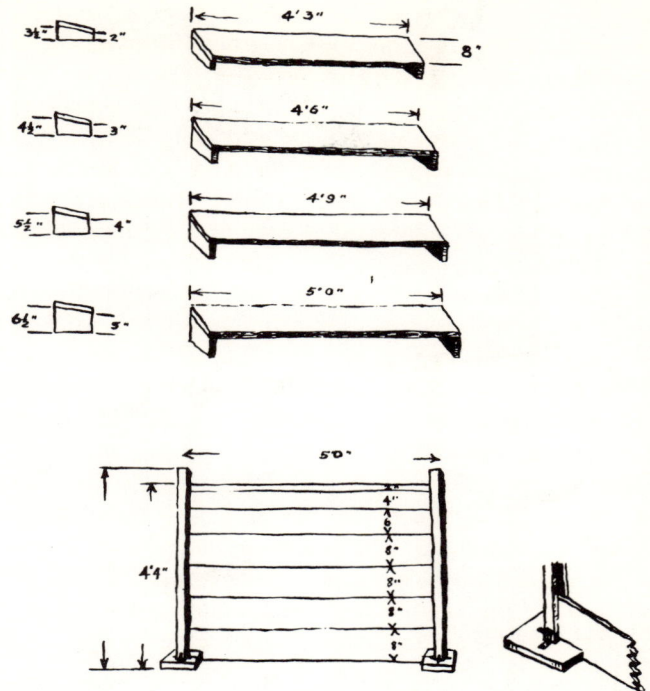

Broad jump and solid hurdle.

In Open competition, the dog must perform such exercises as heeling free, the drop on recall, and the retrieve on the flat and over the high jump. Also, he must execute the broad jump, and the long sit and long down.

In the Utility class, competition includes scent discrimination, the directed retrieve, the signal exercise, directed jumping, and the group examination.

Tracking is the most difficult test. It is always done out-of-doors, of course, and, for obvious reasons, cannot be held at a dog show. The dog must follow a scent trail that is about a quarter mile in length. He is also required to find a scent object (glove, wallet, or other article) left by a stranger who has walked the course to lay down the scent. The dog is required to follow the trail a half to two hours after the scent is laid.

An ideal way to train a dog for obedience competition is to join an obedience class or a training club. In organized class work, beginners' classes cover pretty much the same exercises as those

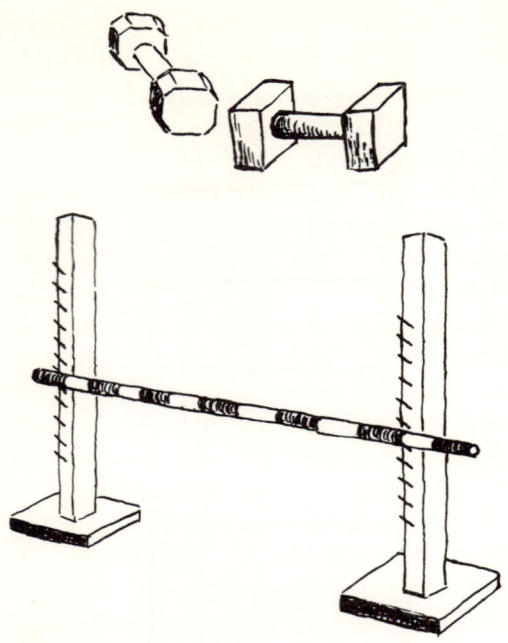

Dumbbells and bar jump.

described in the chapter on training. However, through class work you will develop greater precision than is possible in training your dog by yourself. Amateur handlers often cause the dog to be penalized, for if the handler fails to abide by the rules, it is the dog that suffers the penalty. A common infraction of the rules is using more than one signal or command where regulations stipulate only one may be used. Classwork will help eliminate such errors, which the owner may make unconsciously if he is working alone. Working with a class will also acquaint both dog and handler with ring procedure so that obedience trials will not present unforeseen problems.

Thirty or forty owners and dogs often comprise a class, and exercises are performed in unison, with individual instruction provided if it is required. The procedure followed in training—in fact, even wording of various commands—may vary from instructor to instructor. Equipment used will vary somewhat, also, but will usually include a training collar and leash such as those shown on page 109, a long line, a dumbbell, and a jumping stick.

The latter may be a short length of heavy doweling or a broom handle and both it and the dumbbell are usually painted white for increased visibility.

A bitch in season must never be taken to a training class, so before enrolling a female dog, you should determine whether she may be expected to come into season before classes are scheduled to end. If you think she will, it is better to wait and enroll her in a later course, rather than start the course and then miss classes for several weeks.

In addition to the time devoted to actual work in class, the dog must have regular, daily training sessions for practice at home. Before each class or home training session, the dog should be exercised so he will not be highly excited when the session starts, and he must be given an opportunity to relieve himself before the session begins. (Should he have an accident during the class, it is your responsibility to clean up after him.) The dog should be fed several hours before time for the class to begin or else after the class is over—never just before going to class.

If you decide to enter your dog in obedience competition, it is well to enter a small, informal show the first time. Dogs are usually called in the order in which their names appear in the catalog, so as soon as you arrive at the show, acquaint yourself with the schedule. If your dog is not the first to be judged, spend some time at ringside, observing the routine so you will know what to expect when your dog's turn comes.

In addition to collar, leash, and other equipment, you should take your dog's food and water pans and a supply of the food and water to which he is accustomed. You should also take his brushes and combs in order to give him a last-minute brushing before you enter the ring. It is important that the dog look his best even though he isn't to be judged on his appearance.

Before entering the ring, exercise your dog, give him a drink of water, and permit him to relieve himself. Once your dog enters the ring, give him your full attention and be sure to give voice commands distinctly so he will hear and understand, for there will be many distractions at ringside.

Top dogs in Utility Class. This illustrates variety of breeds that compete in obedience.

Genetics

Genetics, the science of heredity, deals with the processes by which physical and mental traits of parents are transmitted to offspring. For centuries, man has been trying to solve these puzzles, but only in the last two hundred years has significant progress been made.

During the eighteenth century, Kölreuter, a German scientist, made revolutionary discoveries concerning plant sexuality and hybridization but was unable to explain just how hereditary processes worked. In the middle of the nineteenth century, Gregor Johann Mendel, an Augustinian monk, experimented with the ordinary garden pea and made other discoveries of major significance. He found that an inherited characteristic was inherited as a complete unit, and that certain characteristics predominated over others. Next, he observed that the hereditary characteristics of each parent are contained in each offspring, even when they are not visible, and that "hidden" characteristics can be transferred without change in their nature to the grandchildren, or even later generations. Finally, he concluded that although heredity contains an element of uncertainty, some things are predictable on the basis of well-defined mathematical laws.

Unfortunately, Mendel's published paper went unheeded, and when he died in 1884 he was still virtually unknown to the scientific world. But other researchers were making discoveries, too. In 1900, three different scientists reported to learned societies that much of their research in hereditary principles had been proved years before by Gregor Mendel and that findings matched perfectly.

Thus, hereditary traits were proved to be transmitted through the chromosomes found in pairs in every living being, one of each pair contributed by the mother, the other by the father. Within each chromosome have been found hundreds of smaller structures, or genes, which are the actual determinants of hereditary characteristics. Some genes are dominant and will be seen in the offspring. Others are recessive and will not be outwardly apparent, yet can be passed on to the offspring to combine with a similar recessive gene of the other parent and thus be seen. Or they may be passed on to the offspring, not be outwardly apparent, but be passed on again to become apparent in a later generation.

Once the genetic theory of inheritance became widely known, scientists began drawing a well-defined line between inheritance and environment. More recent studies show some overlapping of these influences and indicate a combination of the two may be responsible for certain characteristics. For instance, studies have proved that extreme cold increases the amount of black pigment in the skin and hair of the "Himalayan" rabbit, although it has little or no effect on the white or colored rabbit. Current research also indicates that even though characteristics are determined by the genes, some environmental stress occurring at a particular period of pregnancy might cause physical change in the embryo.

Long before breeders had any knowledge of genetics, they practiced one of its most important principles—selective breeding. Experience quickly showed that "like begets like," and by breeding like with like and discarding unlike offspring, the various individual breeds were developed to the point where variations were relatively few. Selective breeding is based on the idea of maintaining the quality of a breed at the highest possible level, while improving whatever defects are prevalent. It requires that only the top dogs in a litter be kept for later breeding, and that inferior specimens be ruthlessly eliminated.

In planning any breeding program, the first requisite is a definite goal—that is, to have clearly in mind a definite picture of the type of dog you wish eventually to produce. To attempt to breed perfection is to approach the problem unrealistically. But if you don't breed for improvement, it is preferable that you not breed at all.

As a first step, you should select a bitch that exemplifies as many of the desired characteristics as possible and mate her with a dog that also has as many of the desired characteristics as possible. If you start with mediocre pets, you will produce mediocre pet puppies. If you decide to start with more than one bitch, all should closely approach the type you desire, since you will

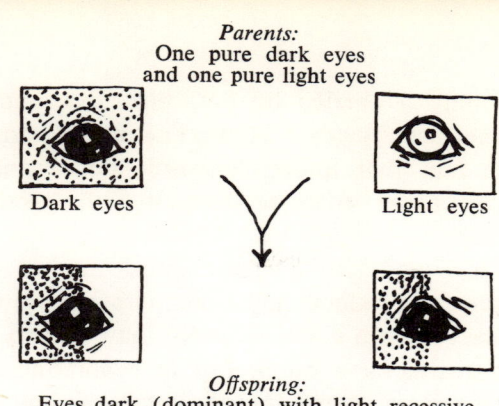

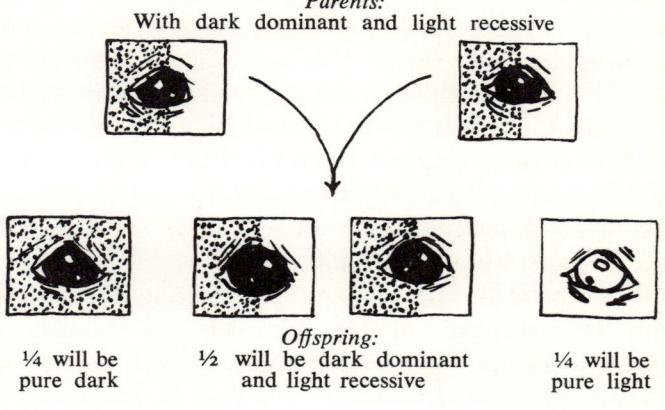

The above is a schematic representation of the Mendelian law as it applies to the inheritance of eye color. The law applies in the same way to the inheritance of other physical characteristics.

then stand a better chance of producing uniformly good puppies from all. Breeders often start with a single bitch and keep the best bitches in every succeeding generation.

Experienced breeders look for "prepotency" in breeding stock —that is, the ability of a dog or bitch to transmit traits to most or all of its offspring. While the term is usually used to describe the transmission of good qualities, a dog may also be prepotent in transmitting faults. To be prepotent in a practical sense, a dog must possess many characteristics controlled by dominant genes. If desired characteristics are recessive, they will be apparent in the offspring only if carried by both sire and dam. Prepotent dogs and bitches usually come from a line of prepotent ancestors, but the mere fact that a dog has exceptional ancestors will not necessarily mean that he himself will produce exceptional offspring.

A single dog may sire a tremendous number of puppies, whereas a bitch can produce only a comparatively few litters during her lifetime. Thus, a sire's influence may be very widespread as compared to that of a bitch. But in evaluating a particular litter, it must be remembered that the bitch has had as much influence as has had the dog.

Inbreeding, line-breeding, outcrossing, or a combination of the three are the methods commonly used in selective breeding.

Inbreeding is the mating together of closely related animals, such as father-daughter, mother-son, or brother-sister. Although some breeders insist such breeding will lead to the production of defective individuals, it is through rigid inbreeding that all breeds of dogs have been established. Controlled tests have shown that any harmful effects appear within the first five or ten generations, and that if rigid selection is exercised from the beginning, a vigorous inbred strain will be built up.

Line-breeding is also the mating together of individuals related by family lines. However, matings are made not so much on the basis of the dog's and bitch's relationship to each other, but, instead, on the basis of their relationship to a highly admired ancestor, with a view to perpetuating his qualities. Line-breeding constitutes a long-range program and cannot be accomplished in a single generation.

Outcrossing is the breeding together of two dogs that are unrelated in family lines. Actually, since breeds have been developed through the mating of close relatives, all dogs within any given breed are related to some extent. There are few breedings that are true outcrosses, but if there is no common ancestor within five generations, a mating is usually considered an outcross.

Experienced breeders sometimes outcross for one generation in order to eliminate a particular fault, then go back to inbreeding or line-breeding. Neither the good effects nor the bad effects of outcrossing can be truly evaluated in a single mating, for undesirable recessive traits may be introduced into a strain, yet not show up for several generations. Outcrossing is better left to experienced breeders, for continual outcrossing results in a wide variation in type and great uncertainty as to the results that may be expected.

Two serious defects that are believed heritable—subluxation and orchidism—should be zealously guarded against, and afflicted dogs and their offspring should be eliminated from breeding programs. Subluxation is a condition of the hip joint where the bone of the socket is eroded and the head of the thigh bone is also worn away, causing lameness which becomes progressively more serious until the dog is unable to walk. Orchidism is the failure of one or both testicles to develop and descend properly. When one testicle is involved, the term "monorchid" is used. When both are involved, "cryptorchid" is used. A cryptorchid is almost always sterile, whereas a monorchid is usually fertile. There is evidence that orchidism "runs in families" and that a monorchid transmits the tendency through bitch and male puppies alike.

Through the years, many misconceptions concerning heredity have been perpetuated. Perhaps the one most widely perpetuated is the idea evolved hundreds of years ago that somehow characteristics were passed on through the mixing of the blood of the parents. We still use terminology evolved from that theory when we speak of bloodlines, or describe individuals as full-blooded, despite the fact that the theory was disproved more than a century ago.

Also inaccurate and misleading is any statement that a definite fraction or proportion of an animal's inherited characteristics can be positively attributed to a particular ancestor. Individuals lacking knowledge of genetics sometimes declare that an individual receives half his inherited characteristics from each parent, a quarter from each grandparent, an eighth from each great-grandparent, etc. Thousands of volumes of scientific findings have been published, but no simple way has been found to determine positively which characteristics have been inherited from which ancestors, for the science of heredity is infinitely complex.

Any breeder interested in starting a serious breeding program should study several of the excellent books on canine genetics that are currently available.

Whelping box. Detail at right shows proper side-wall construction which helps keep small puppies confined and provides sheltered nook which to prevent crushing or smothering.

Breeding and Whelping

The breeding life of a bitch begins when she comes into season the first time at the age of about one to two years (depending on what breed she is). Thereafter, she will come in season at roughly six-month intervals, but this, too, is subject to variation. Her maximum fertility builds up from puberty to full maturity and then declines until a state of total sterility is reached in old age. Just when this occurs is hard to determine, for the fact that an older bitch shows signs of being in season doesn't necessarily mean she is still capable of reproducing.

The length of the season varies from eighteen to twenty-one days. The first indication is a pronounced swelling of the vulva with coincidental bleeding (called "showing color") for about the first seven to nine days. The discharge gradually turns to a creamy color, and it is during this phase (estrus), from about the tenth to the fifteenth days, that the bitch is ovulating and is receptive to the male. The ripe, unfertilized ova survive for about seventy-two hours. If fertilization doesn't occur, the ova die and are discharged the next time the bitch comes in season. If fertilization does take place, each ovum attaches itself to the walls of the uterus, a membrane forms to seal it off, and a foetus develops from it.

Following the estrus phase, the bitch is still in season until about the twenty-first day and will continue to be attractive to males, although she will usually fight them off as she did the first few days. Nevertheless, to avoid accidental mating, the bitch must be confined for the entire period. Virtual imprisonment is necessary, for male dogs display uncanny abilities in their efforts to reach a bitch in season.

The odor that attracts the males is present in the bitch's urine, so it is advisable to take her a good distance from the house before permitting her to relieve herself. To eliminate problems completely, your veterinarian can prescribe a preparation that will disguise the odor but will not interfere with breeding when the time is right. Many fanciers use such preparations when exhibiting a bitch and find that nearby males show no interest whatsoever. But it is not advisable to permit a bitch to run loose when she has been given a product of this type, for during estrus she will seek the company of male dogs and an accidental mating may occur.

A potential brood bitch, regardless of breed, should have good bone, ample breadth and depth of ribbing, and adequate room in the pelvic region. Unless a bitch is physically mature—well beyond the puppy stage when she has her first season—breeding should be delayed until her second or a later season. Furthermore, even though it is possible for a bitch to conceive twice a year, she should not be bred oftener than once a year. A bitch that is bred too often will age prematurely and her puppies are likely to lack vigor.

Two or three months before a bitch is to be mated, her physical condition should be considered carefully. If she is too thin, provide a rich, balanced diet plus the regular exercise needed to develop strong, supple muscles. Daily exercise on the lead is as necessary for the too-thin bitch as for the too fat one, although the latter will need more exercise and at a brisker pace, as well as a reduction of food, if she is to be brought to optimum condition. A prospective brood bitch must have had permanent distemper shots as well as rabies vaccination. And a month before her season is due, a veterinarian should examine a stool specimen for worms. If there is evidence of infestation, the bitch should be wormed.

A dog may be used at stud from the time he reaches physical maturity, well on into old age. The first time your bitch is bred, it is well to use a stud that has already proven his ability by having sired other litters. The fact that a neighbor's dog is readily available should not influence your choice, for to produce the best puppies, you must select the stud most suitable from a genetic standpoint.

If the stud you prefer is not going to be available at the time your bitch is to be in season, you may wish to consult your veterinarian concerning medications available for inhibiting the onset of the season. With such preparations, the bitch's season can be delayed indefinitely.

Usually the first service will be successful. However, if it isn't, in most cases an additional service is given free, provided the stud dog is still in the possession of the same owner. If the bitch misses, it may be because her cycle varies widely from normal. Through microscopic examination, a veterinarian can determine exactly when the bitch is entering the estrus phase and thus is likely to conceive.

The owner of the stud should give you a stud-service certificate, providing a four-generation pedigree for the sire and showing the date of mating. The litter registration application is completed only after the puppies are whelped, but it, too, must be signed by the owner of the stud as well as the owner of the bitch. Registration forms may be secured by writing The American Kennel Club.

In normal pregnancy there is usually visible enlargement of the abdomen by the end of the fifth week. By palpation (feeling with the fingers) a veterinarian may be able to distinguish developing puppies as early as three weeks after mating, but it is unwise for a novice to poke and prod, and try to detect the presence of unborn puppies.

The gestation period normally lasts nine weeks, although it may vary from sixty-one to sixty-five days. If it goes beyond sixty-five days from the date of mating, a veterinarian should be consulted.

During the first four or five weeks, the bitch should be permitted her normal amount of activity. As she becomes heavier, she should be walked on the lead, but strenuous running and jumping should be avoided. Her diet should be well balanced (see page 43), and if she should become constipated, small amounts of mineral oil may be added to her food.

A whelping box should be secured about two weeks before the puppies are due, and the bitch should start then to use it as her bed so she will be accustomed to it by the time puppies arrive. Preferably, the box should be square, with each side long enough so that the bitch can stretch out full length and have several inches to spare at either end. The bottom should be padded with an old cotton rug or other material that is easily laundered. Edges of the padding should be tacked to the floor of the box so the puppies will not get caught in it and smother. Once it is obvious labor is about to begin, the padding should be covered with several layers of spread-out newspapers. Then, as papers become soiled, the top layer can be pulled off, leaving the area clean.

Forty-eight to seventy-two hours before the litter is to be whelped, a definite change in the shape of the abdomen will be noted. Instead of looking barrel-shaped, the abdomen will sag pendulously. Breasts usually redden and become enlarged, and milk may be present a day or two before the puppies are whelped. As the time becomes imminent, the bitch will probably scratch and root at her bedding in an effort to make a nest, and will refuse food and ask to be let out every few minutes. But the surest sign is a drop in temperature of two or three degrees about twelve hours before labor begins.

The bitch's abdomen and flanks will contract sharply when labor actually starts, and for a few minutes she will attempt to expel a puppy, then rest for a while and try again. Someone should stay with the bitch the entire time whelping is taking place, and if she appears to be having unusual difficulties, a veterinarian should be called.

Puppies are usually born head first, though some may be born feet first and no difficulty encountered. Each puppy is enclosed in a separate membranous sac that the bitch will remove with her teeth. She will sever the umbilical cord, which will be attached to the soft, spongy afterbirth that is expelled right after the puppy emerges. Usually the bitch eats the afterbirth, so it is necessary to watch and make sure one is expelled for each puppy whelped. If afterbirth is retained, the bitch may develop peritonitis and die.

The dam will lick and nuzzle each newborn puppy until it is warm and dry and ready to nurse. If puppies arrive so close together that she can't take care of them, you can help her by rubbing the puppies dry with a soft cloth. If several have been whelped but the bitch continues to be in labor, all but one should be removed and placed in a small box lined with clean towels and warmed to about seventy degrees. The bitch will be calmer if one puppy is left with her at all times.

Whelping sometimes continues as long as twenty-four hours for a very large litter, but a litter of two or three puppies may be whelped in an hour. When the bitch settles down, curls around the puppies and nuzzles them to her, it usually indicates that all have been whelped.

The bitch should be taken away for a few minutes while you clean the box and arrange clean padding. If her coat is soiled, sponge it clean before she returns to the puppies. Once she is back in the box, offer her a bowl of warm beef broth and a pan of cool water, placing both where she will not have to get up in order to reach them. As soon as she indicates interest in food, give her a generous bowl of chopped meat to which codliver oil and dicalcium phosphate have been added (see page 43).

If inadequate amounts of calcium are provided during the period the puppies are nursing, eclampsia may develop. Symptoms are violent trembling, rapid rise in temperature, and rigidity of muscles. Veterinary assistance must be secured immediately, for death may result in a very short time. Treatment consists of massive doses of calcium gluconate administered intravenously, after which symptoms subside in a miraculously short time.

All puppies are born blind and their eyes open when they are ten to fourteen days old. At first the eyes have a bluish cast and appear weak, and the puppies must be protected from strong light until at least ten days after the eyes open.

To ensure proper emotional development, young dogs should be shielded from loud noises and rough handling. Being lifted by the front legs is painful and may result in permanent injury to the shoulders. So when lifting a puppy, always place one hand under the chest with the forefinger between the front legs, and place the other hand under his bottom.

Sometimes the puppies' nails are so long and sharp that they scratch the bitch's breasts. Since the nails are soft, they can be trimmed with ordinary scissors.

If of a breed that ordinarily has a docked tail, puppies should have their tails shortened when they are three days old. Dewclaws—thumblike appendages appearing on the inside of the legs of some breeds—are removed at the same time. While both are simple procedures, they shouldn't be attempted by amateurs.

In certain breeds it is customary to crop the ears, also. This should be done at about eight weeks of age. Cropping should never be attempted by anyone other than a veterinarian, for it requires use of anesthesia and knowledge of surgical techniques, as well as judgment as to the eventual size of the dog and proportion of ear to be removed so the head will be balanced when the dog is mature.

At about four weeks of age, formula should be provided. The amount fed each day should be increased over a period of two weeks, when the puppies can be weaned completely. The formula should be prepared as described on page 41, warmed to lukewarm, and poured into a shallow pan placed on the floor of the box. After his mouth has been dipped into the mixture a few times, a puppy will usually start to lap formula. All puppies should be allowed to eat from the same pan, but be sure the small ones get their share. If they are pushed aside, feed them separately. Permit the puppies to nurse part of the time, but gradually increase the number of meals of formula. By the time the puppies are five weeks old, the dam should be allowed with them only at night. When they are about six weeks old, they should be weaned completely and fed the puppy diet described on page 41.

Once they are weaned, puppies should be given temporary distemper injections every two weeks until they are old enough for permanent inoculations. At six weeks, stool specimens should be checked for worms, for almost without exception, puppies become infested. Specimens should be checked again at eight weeks, and as often thereafter as your veterinarian recommends.

Sometimes owners decide as a matter of convenience to have a bitch spayed or a male castrated. While this is recommended when a dog has a serious inheritable defect or when abnormalities of reproductive organs develop, in sound, normal purebred dogs, spaying a bitch or castrating a male may prove a definite disadvantage. The operations automatically bar dogs from competing in shows as well as precluding use for breeding. The operations are seldom dangerous, but they should not be performed without good reason.

Winning Miniature Schnauzers

The following lists of winning Miniature Schnauzers cover a period of two and one-half decades. Included are four well-known dog shows that help to indicate the increasing magnitude of Miniature Schnauzer participation over the years. Each listing gives the year the show was held, the number of dogs in competition, the name of the judge who selected the winners, and the names of the winning dogs and their owners.

It is to be remembered that the shows listed represent only a small segment of the total competition in dog shows held across the country, and that many exceptionally fine dogs therefore go unmentioned.

The shows chosen for this listing include two American Miniature Schnauzer Club Specialty Shows (one of which is held in conjunction with the Montgomery County Kennel Club Show now held in Penlynn, Pennsylvania, in October; the other held in conjunction with the Combined Terrier Specialty Show in New York City in February), the Westminster Kennel Club Show (held in Madison Square Garden in New York City in February), and the International Kennel Club Show (held in Chicago in April). Each of these shows has a long and proud history. All are supported and attended by the dog fancy from all areas of the nation.

Left to right: Danial, Madam, Kappy, Arabella, Rickey, Ringer, Blackjack (back), and Little Sue Sue.

Can. Ch. Sylva Sprite Satchmo Sent Me.

Ch. Fancway's Lingo at two years of age.

American Miniature Schnauzer Club Specialty
Held in February — New York

Year—Dogs in competition—Judge	Winners		Owners
1973 — 85 E. Bracy	BB: BOS: WD: WB:	Ch. Carolane's Royal Rogue Valharra's Dubarry Bardon's Jiffy Pop Valharra's Dubarry	J. Heilshorn H. Quick M. Roberts H. Quick
1972 — 95 A. Rosenberg	BB: BOS: WD: WB:	Ch. Kazel's Favorite Blockley Mischievous Imp Penlan Paperboy Blockley Mischievous Imp	Church Dunner Hirstein Dunner
1971 — 76 P. Roberts	BB: BOS: WD: WB:	Ch. Cristy Lee's Frosty Jack Ch. Wynmore Summer Song Travelmor's Best Friend Schalltrichter's Schnickel	Hendricks Seaberg Moore Beauchamp
1970 — 73 L. E. Murray	BB: BOS: WD: WB:	Ch. Mankit's To The Moon Ch. Blythewood Her Highness Cristy Lee's Frosty Jack Janco's Dixie	E. Miller Lewis Hendricks Boyd
1969 — 94 A. Rosenberg	BB: BOS: WD: WB:	Ch. Mankit's To The Moon Ch. Miown Exotic Poppy Ziegerwald Zacotan BoTurn Fancie of Harga	E. Miller Laughter Lutz Cederberg

Marcheim Rufus V. Etheredge at 12 weeks of age.

Tucker Grayfriar, UD, a top obedience dog.

Jonaire Pocono Black Satin. First black ever to get points. Breeder-owner, Jonaire Kennels.

Year—Dogs in competition—Judge		Winners	Owners
1968 — 82	BB:	Ch. Blythewood Chief Bosun	Huber
J. T. Marvin	BOS:	Ch. Howtwo's Harlequin	Hardgrave/Owen
	WD:	Orbit's Time Traveler	Cazier
	WB:	Blythewood Sweet Velvet	Huber
1967 — 77	BB:	Ch. Landmark's Masterpiece	Weidlein
Mrs. M. A. Anspach	BOS:	Luvemal's Bedazzling	Stacy
	WD:	Zomerhof's Ruffy Ringo	Somers
	WB:	Luvemal's Bedazzling	Stacy
1966 — 89	BB:	Ch. Blythewood Chief Bosun	Huber
A. Rosenberg	BOS:	Ch. Winsomor Miss Kitty	Halpern
	WD:	Rujax Royal Randy	J. & R. Miller
	WB:	Crown Post Connie's Caper	Crown Post Kls.
1965 — 81	BB:	Ch. Blythewood Main Gazebo	Huber
L. J. Murr	BOS:	Ch. Janhof's Bon Bon of Adford	Cazier
	WD:	Pfulhan's Friar Tuck	Getzendanner
	WB:	Pat-Je's Christy Lee	Hendricks
1964 — 80	BB:	Orlong's Lisa Lou	Hendricks
P. Roberts	BOS:	Ch. Blythewood Main Gazebo	Huber
	WD:	Mutiny Lil Old Winemaker Me	Hall
	WB:	Orlong's Lisa Lou	Hendricks

Ch. Fancway's Lingo at age of two months (whelped 1958).

Ch. Mankit's Dashing Dennis, sire of seven AKC champions, including two multiple Best-in-Show winners.

Year—Dogs in competition—Judge	Winners		Owners
1963 — 73 Miss D. Williams	BB: BOS: WD: WB:	Geelong Enchanting Miss Ch. Yankee Squadron Leader Top Notch Crescendo Geelong Enchanting Miss	Travelmor Kls. O. Moore Bowen Travelmor Kls.
1962 — 60 A. Rosenberg	BB: BOS: WD: WB:	Ch. Luvemal's Master Copy Ch. Miss Maxine of Crestwood Park Jonaire Pocono Gladiator Helarry's Danielle	Stacy Deaver & Salkowitz Marriott Austin
1961 — 79 W. L. Kendrick	BB: BOS: WD: WB:	Trayhom Tramp a Bout Ch. Blythewood Touch of Silver Trayhom Tramp a Bout Mankit's Alfreda	W. & T. Miller Bauernschmidt W. & T. Miller K. Miller
1960 — 62 G. H. Hartman	BB: BOS: WD: WB:	Ch. Yankee Pride Col. Stump Gunlad Prelude Phil-Mar Impressive Lover Gunlad Prelude	Sailer Ladensack Walsh/Smith Ladensack
1959 — 44 R. A. Kerns, Jr.	BB: BOS: WD: WB:	Ch. Yankee Pride Col. Stump Jonaire Honey in the Evenin Wilkern's by Jingo Jonaire Honey in the Evenin	Sailer Jonaire Kls. Daks Jonaire Kls.

Jonaire entry at Westminster, 1957. Left to right: Ch. J. P. High Class, J. P. Talisman, Ch. J. P. Smart Money, Ch. J. P. Smart Cookie, Ch. J. P. Blue Print. All bred and owned by Jonaire Kennels.

Year—Dogs in competition—Judge	Winners		Owners
1958 — 58 P. Roberts	BB:	Ch. Perci Bee's First Impression	Shelley
	BOS:	Janco Merri Ann	Janco Kls.
	WD:	Eleazer of Marienhof	Marienhof Kls.
	WB:	Janco Merri Ann	Janco Kls.
1957 — 69 A. Rosenberg	BB:	Ch. Benrook Brandy	Benrook Kls.
	BOS:	Sandown's Honey Babe	Willow Lawn Kls
	WD:	Yankee Pride Ringmaster	Sailer
	WB:	Sandown's Honey Babe	Willow Lawn Kls
1956 — 60 H. J. Sayres	BB:	Ch. Benrook Randy	Vann
	BOS:	Trayhom Terrific	W. & T. Miller
	WD:	Marwyck Pitt Penn Lineman	Beard
	WB:	Dorem Blue Angel	Getz
1955 — 46 W. L. Kendrick	BB:	Ch. Benrook Randy	Benrook Kls.
	BOS:	Ch. Handful's Pheasant	Simmonds
	WD:	Betty's Storm	Laventhall
	WB:	Delheath Gay Lucy	D. Heath
1954 — 36 M. Silver	BB:	Cecile of Flint Hill	Johnston
	BOS:	Ch. Phil-Mar's Gay Knight	Anspach
	WD:	Cosburn's Esquire	Graziano
	WB:	Cecile of Flint Hill	Johnston
1953 — 38 Mrs. Marie E. Slattery	BB:	Dorem Favorite	Dorem Kls.
	BOS:	Ch. Forest Nod of Mandeville	Jenner
	WD:	Dorem Favorite	Dorem Kls.
	WB:	Benrook Ben Gay	Kantor

Year—Dogs in competition—Judge	Winners		Owners
1952 — 38 R. A. Kerns, Jr.	BB: BOS: WD: WB:	Ch. Benrook Buckaroo Ch. Marnan's Hi Jinks Benrook Bryce Wilkern Pepper Pot	Benrook Kls. Evans Benrook Kls. Cooper
1951 — 39 E. A. Sayres	BB: BOS: WD: WB:	Ch. Dorem Tribute Benrook Bona Benrook Benhow Benrook Bona	Williams/Daks Benrook Kls. Benrook Kls. Benrook Kls.
1950 — 40 P. Talmage	BB: BOS: WD: WB:	Ch. Dorem Inspiration Ch. Dorem Tribute Destiny of Ledahof Wilkern Ado	Williams Williams/Daks Storch Wilkern Kls.
1949 — 32 F. Downing	BB: BOS: WD: WB:	Ch. Dorem Delegate Ch. Sorceress of Ledahof Discovery of Marienhof Meldon's Manana	D. Williams Evashwick Sailer Benrook Kls.
1948 — 22 Mrs. E. A. Dalton	BB: BOS: WD: WB:	Ch. Dorem Display Ch. Katydid of Marienhof Meldon's Misty of Eldonhof Dorem Heather of Eldonhof	Meldon Constable Meldon Dorem Kls.
1947 — 27 Mrs. J. M. Deaver	BB: BOS: WD: WB:	Dorem Display Ch. Enchantress Dorem Tribute Karen of Marienhof	Meldon Gadd Meldon Rooks

Ch. Allaruth's Jade

American Miniature Schnauzer Club Specialty
Now held in October — Pennsylvania

Year—Dogs in competition—Judge	Winners		Owners
1972 — 106 R. J. Moore	BB: BOS: WD: WB:	Ch. Kazel's Favorite Ch. Whim Cin's Mia Maria Jankell's Torgau Shiril's Pride of Devi	Church Hallock Haskell Gluntz
1971 — 77 Miss G. Simmonds	BB: BOS: WD: WB:	Ch. Sky Rocket's Uproar Carolane's Pixie Princess Sky Rocket's Upswing Carolane's Pixie Princess	Ferguson/Hoehn Emden Smith Emden
1970 — 116 Mrs. J. E. Clark	BB: BOS: WD: WB:	Ch. Marcheim Helza Poppin Ch. Andrel's Romance Andrel's Reliance Blythewood Hurrah for Edith	Congdon/Snobel Czapski Czapski Huber
1969 — 113 R. J. Moore	BB: BOS: WD: WB:	Ch. Mankit's To The Moon Penlan Prelude To Victory Mankit's Thar He Goes Penlan Prelude To Victory	E. Miller Hirstein Thomann Hirstein

Ch. Carrousel Lafitte, 1967. (Photo by William P. Gilbert.)

Year—Dogs in competition—Judge	Winners		Owners
1968 — 92 H. R. Hartley	BB: BOS: WD: WB:	Mankit's To The Moon Penlan Paramour Mankit's To The Moon Penlan Paramour	E. Miller Dunson E. Miller Dunson
1967 — 91 P. Roberts	BB: BOS: WD: WB:	Ch. Travelmor's Witchcraft Andrel's Ovation Blythewood Blue Max Andrel's Ovation	W. Moore Czapski Huber Czapski
1966 — 102 C. O. Taylor	BB: BOS: WD: WB:	Ch. Mankit's Signal Go Miown Erick's Hi Hope Landmark's Masterpiece Miown Erick's Hi Hope	E. Miller Laughter Weidlein Laughter
1965 — 105 T. H. Carruthers	BB: BOS: WD: WB:	Ch. Mankit's Signal Go Jasper's Beau Catcher Susie Major Charmer Jasper's Beau Catcher Susie	E. Miller Wilson Pagano E. Wilson
1964 — 83 N. Daks	BB: BOS: WD: WB:	Ch. Mankit's Signal Go Phil-Mar Lucky Susan Blythewood Chief Bosun Phil-Mar Lucky Susan	E. Miller Anspach Huber Anspach

Lady Gretchen Frost, CDX

Ch. Jonaire Pocono Top Scholar. Best of Breed, Westminster, 1965.

Year—Dogs in competition—Judge	Winners		Owners
1963 — 75 G. H. Hartman	BB: BOS: WD: WB:	Ch. Phil-Mar Dark Knight Ch. Mankit's Katrina Geelong Royal Playboy Rik-Rak Rock Candy	Anspach D. Miller Geelong Kls. Ackerman
1962 — 73 J. W. Trullinger	BB: BOS: WD: WB:	Ch. Magic of Sparks Ch. Top Notch Winsome Winnie Travelmor's Beach Boy Geelong Enchanting Miss	Sailer Hardie W. Moore Geelong Kls.
1961 — 68 Mrs. L. B. Martin	BB: BOS: WD: WB:	Ch. Luvemal's Master Copy Helarry's Jeanne Andrel's Debonaire Helarry's Jeanne	Stacy Austin Czapski Austin
1960 — 69 P. Roberts	BB: BOS: WD: WB:	Ch. Phil-Mar Lugar Ch. Blythewood Touch of Silver Hans of Abrolee Sparks Tinkerbell	Anspach Bauernschmidt Sailer Deaver

Black and silver litter whelped March 23, 1971. Dam, Mio's Miss Twilight. Sire, Ch. Tiger Bo Von-Riptide. Photo at 2½ months of age.

Ch. Blythewood His Majesty, sire of 9 champions. Winners Dog, Westminster, 1968.

Year—Dogs in competition—Judge		Winners	Owners
1959 — 64 N. Daks	BB: BOS: WD: WB:	Ch. Yankee Pride Col. Stump Ch. Jonaire Honey in the Evenin Luvemal's Gentleman Gim Rik Rak Regina	Sailer Jonaire Kls. Luvemal Kls. Guest Lane Kls
1958 — 43 L. S. Worden	BB: BOS: WD: WB:	Ch. Blythewood Merry Maker Ch. Yankee Pride Col. Stump Handful's Popper Luvemal's Carbon Copy	Delfin Kls. Sailer Czapski Stacy
1957 — 37 Miss D. Williams	BB: BOS: WD: WB:	Ch. Perci Bee's First Impression Bilco's Chandelle Glenshaw's Johnny Appleseed Bilco's Chandelle	Shelley Condon Snowden Condon
1956 — 37 Mrs. M. Slattery	BB: BOS: WD: WB:	Yankee Pride Ring Master Ch. Dorem Originality Yankee Pride Ring Master Phil-Mar Miss Maggie	Babisch Dorem Kls. Babisch Anspach

Like father, like son! Ch. Travelmor's Fantazio and Ch. Travelmor's Rango, sons of Ch. Travelmor's Witchcraft.

Mrs. Olive Davis Moore and Ch. Travelmor's Witchcraft. Bill Moore with Ch. Travelmor's Gay Blade, sire of Witchcraft.

Ch. Jonaire Pocono Top-Hit

Year—Dogs in competition—Judge	Winners		Owners
1955 — 53 F. B. Brumby	BB: BOS: WD: WB:	Dody's Dimitri Dorem Blue Angel Dody's Dimitri Dorem Blue Angel	Goldsworthy Getz Goldsworthy Getz
1954 — 17 Mrs. W. J. Hoos	BB: BOS: WD: WB:	Ch. Cosburn's Esquire Ch. Handful's Pheasant Benrook Rego Fashion of Marienhof	Graziano Simmonds Zorra Simmonds
1953 — C. A. Swartz	BB: BOS: WD: WB:	Ch. Dorem Ovation Ch. Forest Nod of Mandeville Dody's Daguerreotype Marwyck S. D. Cupid	McCosker Jenner Goldsworthy Francis
1952 — 9 Mrs. J. M. Dalton	BB: BOS: WD: WB:	Ch. Diplomat of Marienhof Ballerina of Marienhof Josiah of Marienhof Ballerina of Marienhof	Simmonds Marienhof Kls. Marienhof Kls. Marienhof Kls.

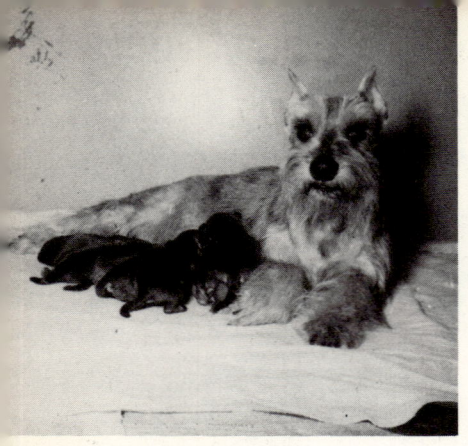

A Jonaire dam and pups.

Year—Dogs in competition—Judge	Winners		Owners
1951 — 14 Mrs. H. L. Woehling	BB:	Ch. Wilkern Fillip	Boggs
	BOS:	Cosburn's Beau Brummel Honey	Patterson
	WD:	Chieftain of Ledahof	Ahern
	WB:	Cosburn's Beau Brummel Honey	Patterson
1950 — 10 A. Mitchell	BB:	Ch. Marwyck Scenery Road	Eremic
	BOS:	Mehitabel of Kenwick	Kenworth
	WD:	Marwyck Brush Cliff	Peterson
	WB:	Mehitabel of Kenwick	Kenworth
1949 — 3 T. P. Phillips	BB:	Brookmeade Sally	Brookmeade Kls.
	BOS:	Chieftain of Ledahof	Dawson
	WD:	Chieftain of Ledahof	Dawson
	WB:	Brookmeade Sally	Brookmeade Kls.
1948 — 4 J. M. Deavers	BB:	Diplomat of Ledahof	Ledahof Kls.
	BOS:	Rachel of Marienhof III	Marienhof Kls.
	WD:	Diplomat of Ledahof	Ledahof Kls.
	WB:	Rachel of Marienhof III	Marienhof Kls.

Marcheim Frosty Blizzard at 12 weeks of age.

Am., Can., Mex. Ch. Fancway's Pirate Jr. of LaMay. WD, 1965 International Kennel Club Show.

Westminster Kennel Club Show
Held in February — New York

Year—Dogs in competition—Judge	Winners		Owners
1973 — 35 J. Murphy	BB: BOS: WD: WB:	Ch. Jankell's Torgau Ch. Whim Cin's Mia Maria Playboy's Block Buster Bazo's Taffy Twist of Baxter	R. & J. Haskell D. Hallock C. Hansen B. Humphries
1972 — 42 Mrs. M. Stephenson	BB: BOS: WD: WB:	Allaruth's Mama's Boy Frosty Jack's Paper Doll Allaruth's Mama's Boy Frosty Jack's Paper Doll	Ziegler Ready Ziegler Ready
1971 — 30 Mrs. P. S. Deaver	BB: BOS: WD: WB:	Valharra's Dionysos Ch. Andrel's Romance Valharra's Dionysos Fontinake's Unique Boutique	Quick Czapski Quick Fontinakes
1970 — 25 N. Daks	BB: BOS: WD: WB:	Ch. Mankit's To The Moon Ch. Unser's Bravo Brava Cristy Lee's Frosty Jack Cristy Lee's Frosty Jill	E. Miller Crews/Fiala Hendricks Hendricks

Am., Can. Ch. Sorceress of Ledahof, whelped 1947. BOS, 1949 American Miniature Schnauzer Club Specialty Show, New York City.

Trayhom Truly Fair, CD, with two of her offspring. (Granddam of Ch. Barclay Square Becky Sharp.)

Year—Dogs in competition—Judge	Winners		Owners
1969 — 29 Mrs. P. M. Silvernail	BB: BOS: WD: WB:	Ch. Mankit's To The Moon Ch. Miown Exotic Poppy Blythewood Page Boy Brandy Lane Thistle Do It	E. Miller Laughter Huttenlock Schwartz
1968 — 24 H. H. Stoecker	BB: BOS: WD: WB:	Ch. Landmark's Masterpiece Ch. Howtwo's Harlequin Blythewood His Majesty Blythewood Sweet Velvet	Weidlein Hardgrave/Owen Huber Huber
1967 — 25 T. P. Bresnahan	BB: BOS: WD: WB:	Ch. Landmark's Masterpiece Luvemal's Bedazzling Uhlan Firebrand Luvemal's Bedazzling	Weidlein Stacy McCarthy Stacy
1966 — 32 R. Waters	BB: BOS: WD: WB:	Delfin Do Donna Ch. Luvemal's Copy Right Luvemal's Ballyhoo Delfin Do Donna	La Bounty Crews Stacy LaBounty
1965 — 29 T. Keator	BB: BOS: WD: WB:	Jonaire Pocono Top Scholar Allaruth's Tweedle Dee Jonaire Pocono Top Scholar Allaruth's Tweedle Dee	Jonaire Kls. Ziegler Jonaire Kls. Ziegler
1964 — 35 J. J. Duncan	BB: BOS: WD: WB:	Orlong's Lisa Lou Ch. Helarry's Harmony Mutiny Lil Old Winemaker Me Orlong's Lisa Lou	Hendricks Cederberg Hall Hendricks

Year—Dogs in competition—Judge	Winners		Owners
1963 — 32 W. H. Ackland	BB: BOS: WD: WB:	Ch. Adford's Bob White Ch. Bilco's Replica Top Notch Crescendo Abingdon Heidi	Hendricks VanHorn Bowen Porter
1962 — 27 R. A. Kerns, Jr.	BB: BOS: WD: WB:	Geelong Big Payoff Helarry's Danielle Geelong Big Payoff Helarry's Danielle	Geelong Kls. Austin Geelong Kls. Austin
1961 — 35 Mrs. P. M. Silvernail	BB: BOS: WD: WB:	Ch. Yankee Pride Col. Stump Ch. Blythewood Touch of Silver Phil-Mar Gay Gunner Grapeside Gloria	Sailer Bauernschmidt Anspach Seamens
1960 — 29 W. R. Proctor	BB: BOS: WD: WB:	Ch. Yankee Pride Col. Stump Ch. Jonaire Honey in the Evenin Jonaire Bucky's Gunsmoke Whimsy of Marienhof II	Sailer Jonaire Kls. Hoagland Marienhof Kls.
1959 — 46 E. B. McKinley	BB: BOS: WD: WB:	Ch. Yankee Pride Col. Stump Phil-Mar Melba Nicomur Cherrio Phil Mar Melba	Sailer Shelley Daks Shelley
1958 — 44 T. Keator	BB: BOS: WD: WB:	Ch. Perci Bee's First Impression Ch. Handful's Silver Pheasant Eleazer of Marienhof Jonaire Pocono Smart Cookie	Shelley Simmonds Marienhof Kls. Jonaire Kls.

Miniature Schnauzer with "friends."

Year—Dogs in competition—Judge	Winners		Owners
1957 — 64 Mrs. A. Riggs IV	BB:	Ch. Dody's Dimitri	Guest Lane Kls.
	BOS:	Ch. Handful's Pheasant	Simmonds
	WD:	Yankee Pride Ringmaster	Sailer
	WB:	Sparks Exotic	Deaver
1956 — 49 G. H. Hartman	BB:	Ch. Benrook Randy	Vann
	BOS:	Trayhom Terrific	W. Miller
	WD:	Allaruth's Attaboy	Ziegler
	WB:	Trayhom Terrific	W. Miller
1955 — 40 Miss D. Williams	BB:	Ch. Phil-Mar's Lucy Lady	Anspach
	BOS:	Ch. Benrook Randy	Benrook Kls.
	WD:	Geelong Playboy	Geelong Kls.
	WB:	Benrook Roselle	Benrook Kls.
1954 — 48 P. N. Silvernail	BB:	Ch. Bursche v Hessen	Loebe
	BOS:	Ch. Benrook Bona	G. Simmonds
	WD:	Wilkern's Second Chance	Mogull
	WB:	Phil Mar's Lucy Lady	Anspach
1953 — 57 Thomas H. Mullins	BB:	Bursche von Hessen	Loebe
	BOS:	Ch. Forest Nod of Mandeville	Jenner
	WD:	Bursche von Hessen	Loebe
	WB:	Dorem Fashion	Dorem Kls.

Ch. Orlong's Lisa Lou, top winner in 1964. BB, 1964 Westminster, and BB, 1964 American Miniature Schnauzer Club Specialty Show, New York. (Photo by Bill Francis.)

Best-in-Show Brace, Ch. Orbit's Agena-B and Ch. Orbit's A-OK of Adford. (Photo by Missy—1968.)

Year—Dogs in competition—Judge	Winners		Owners
1952 — 46 G. H. Hartman	BB:	Ch. Wilkern Fillip	Boggs
	BOS:	Wilkern Pepper Pot	Cooper
	WD:	Benrook Bryce	Benrook Kls.
	WB:	Wilkern Pepper Pot	Cooper
1951 — 38 Mrs. E. A. Dalton	BB:	Benrook Bellona	Benrook Kls.
	BOS:	Ch. Wilkern Adonis	Cooper
	WD:	Benrook Benbow	Benrook Kls.
1950 — 22 J. V. Robinson	BB:	Ch. Mister Chips of Mulberry	Ryan
	BOS:	Ch. Dorem Inspiration	Williams
	WD:	Wilkern Adonis	Wilkern Kls.
	WB:	Wilkern Ado	Wilkern Kls.

Ch. Barclay Square Becky Sharp, BOS, 1966 International Kennel Club Show.

Ch. Ernie of Marienhof, Dick Vaughn handling. Owners, Marienhof Kennels.

Year—Dogs in competition—Judge		Winners	Owners
1949 — 32 Mrs. K. D. Marlatt	BB: BOS: WD: WB:	Ch. Delegate of Ledahof Ch. Katydid of Marienhof Dorem Display Trudy of Kenhoff	Clairedale Kls. Constable Meldon Kalthoff
1948 — 18 Mrs. A. Stone	BB: BOS: WD: WB:	Mister Chips of Mulberry Dorem Diadem Dorem Display Dorem Diadem	Ryan Benrook Kls. Meldon Benrook Kls.
1947 — 5 pts. dogs, 3 pts. bitches C. Shuttleworth	BB: BOS: WD: WB:	Dorem Display Ch. Enchantress Neff's Acclaim Karen of Marienhof	Meldon Gadd Niebank Rooks
1946 — 31 H. Lumb	BB: BOS: WD: WB:	Ch. Sandman of Sharvogue Havahome Freshie Dorem Display Havahome Freshie	Griggs Havahome Kls. Meldon Havahome Kls.

Ch. Blythewood Main Gazebo, a top Best-of-Breed winner, including 1965 American Miniature Schnauzer Club Specialty Show, New York. BOS, 1964 American Miniature Schnauzer Club Specialty Show, New York.

Ch. Hansels Prudence of Marienhof, dam of three champions, shown winning Futurity at American Miniature Schnauzer Club Specialty Show, February 10, 1963.

International Kennel Club Show
Now held in April — Chicago

Year—Dogs in competition—Judge	Winners		Owners
1973 — 61 Mrs. W. Heckmann	BB: BOS: WD: WB: BOW:	Ch. Penlan Checkmate Madeline's Sweet Talk Colonial's Proclamation Madeline's Sweet Talk Colonial's Proclamation	J. Kriegbaum E. & C. Flory L. Pluta E. & C. Flory L. Pluta
1972 — 66 A. P. Knoop	BB: BOS: WD: WB:	Ch. Burn Brae Just Jake Ch. Diandee Born to be Treasured Luremi Winsome Jester Madeline's Sweet Tart	Fields Allen Steinberg Schulz
1971 — 73 F. A. Young	BB: BOS: WD: WB:	Ch. Sky Rocket's Uproar Ch. Bardic Lane's Bakery Lady Pickwick's G. W. Shooting Star Sky Rocket's Dart	Ferguson/Hoehn Walsh Buys MacCarthy
1970 — 60 J. P. Murphy	BB: BOS: WD: WB:	Ch. Mankit's Alex of Dunbar Alpine Baby Ruth Barclay Square Bandersnatch Alpine Baby Ruth	E. Miller Auslander D. Miller Auslander

Am., Can. Ch. Landmark's Masterpiece. BB, 1967 American Miniature Schnauzer Club Specialty Show, New York; WD, 1966 American Miniature Schnauzer Club Specialty, Pennsylvania; BB, 1967 and 1968 Westminster Kennel Club Shows.

Ch. Travelmor's Witchcraft, BB, 1967 American Miniature Schnauzer Club Specialty, Pennsylvania. (Photo by William P. Gilbert.)

Year—Dogs in competition—Judge	Winners		Owners
1969 — 50 H. R. Hartley	BB:	Tammashann's Thunder Cloud	Tomanica
	BOS:	Penlan Protege	Bailey
	WD:	Tammashann's Thunder Cloud	Tomanica
	WB:	Penlan Protege	Bailey
1968 — 77 M. M. Sheppard	BB:	Ch. Mankit's Signal Go	E. Miller
	BOS:	Ch. Orbit's Agena B	Cazier
	WD:	Lou Gin's Avenger	Dunson
	WB:	Abingdon Irresistible	Meiners
1967 — 37 T. A. Kirk	BB:	Ch. Orbit's Space Pilot of Janhof	Schulz
	BOS:	Alpine Patent Pending	Congdon
	WD:	Kanshos Ares	Allcorn
	WB:	Alpine Patent Pending	Congdon
1966 — 65 E. E. Loebe	BB:	Ch. Pickwick's G. W. Kim Kim	Buys
	BOS:	Ch. Barclay Square Becky Sharp	D. Miller
	WD:	The Mariner of Glen Sed	Sedlacek
	WB:	Sparks Hanna	Deaver
1965 — 75 W. L. Kendrick	BB:	Ch. Earldorf Hootenanny	Sobinsky
	BOS:	Moore's Bo Peep	Carman
	WD:	Fancway's Pirate Jr. of LaMay	Fancy
	WB:	Moore's Bo Peep	Carman
1964 — 66 H. R. Hartley	BB:	Ch. Showdown Sherman of Glen Sed	Kendall
	BOS:	Lougin's Cinderella	Hass
	WD:	Mankit's Roust a Bout	Primavera
	WB:	Lougin's Cinderella	Hass

Jonaire Pocono Gretchen, CD, and her puppies. The one in the center took Winners, male, in his first show, and four points.

Ch. Magic of Sparks (a "Colonel Stump" son), BB, American Miniature Schnauzer Club Specialty, October 1962.

Year—Dogs in competition—Judge	Winners		Owners
1963 — 81 W. L. Kendrick	BB: BOS: WD: WB:	Ch. Alex of Earldorf Ch. Dansel's Dutch Treat Phil-Mar Dark Knight Miown Heidi v Brach	Taich Doessel/Lynn Anspach Laughter
1962 — 70 T. Keator	BB: BOS: WD: WB:	Ch. Yankee Pride Col. Stump Ch. Magdolena v Brittanhof Flint Hill Maverick Winsomor Remember Me	Sailer Bailey Johnston McDonald
1961 — 61 G. H. Hartman	BB: BOS: WD: WB:	Brandy the Rock of Glen Sed Ch. Marwyck Belmer Gigi Brandy the Rock of Glen Sed Winsomor Attention Please	Quinlan Sobinsky Quinlan Amato
1960 — 61 E. B. McKinley	BB: BOS: WD: WB:	Ch. Phil-Mar Thunderbolt Andrel's Bonne Amie Jaxown Jack Pot Andrel's Bonne Amie	White Czapski Plouf Czapski

Year—Dogs in competition—Judge		Winners	Owners
1959 — 42 F. B. Brumby	BB: BOS: WD: WB:	Andrel's Viceroy Ch. Gladding's Bie Bie Andrel's Viceroy Jonaire Honey in the Evenin	Czapski E. Miller Czapski Jonaire Kls.
1958 — 33 W. L. Kendrick	BB: BOS: WD: WB:	Ch. Benrook Brandy Gladding's Bie Bie Jonaire Pocono Blue Point Gladding's Bie Bie	Benrook Kls. E. Miller Jonaire Kls. E. Miller
1957 — 40 F. C. Hollander	BB: BOS: WD: WB:	Ch. Benrook Brandy Mirocs Mehitable Ledahof Minim Mirocs Mehitable	Benrook Kls. Graziano Irwin Graziano
1956 — 39 F. Brumby	BB: BOS: WD: WB:	Boxerly of Marienhof Ch. Perci Bee's First Impression Dodi's Dimitri Boxerly of Marienhof	W. H. MacKendrick C. Shelley Guest Lane Kls W. H. MacKendrick

Ch. Mankit's To The Moon, BB, 1969 and 1970 Westminster Kennel Club Shows.

Year—Dogs in competition—Judge	Winners		Owners
1955 — 46 T. C. Hollander	BB: BOS: WD: WB:	Ch. Benrook Randy Lechchen's Adagio Forest Mr. Big Lechchen's Adagio	Vann Armstrong Heinsimer Armstrong
1954 — 30 Mrs. A. Riggs IV	BB: BOS: WD: WB:	Forest Nod of Mandeville Edmarlos Dandee Dude Edmarlos Dandee Dude Belvedere Tribulation	Jenner Frank Frank Claney
1953 — 31 G. Hartman	BB: BOS: WD: WB:	Bursche Von Hassem Ch. Forest Nod of Mandeville Salt & Pepper Sampler Phil-Mar Lady Be Good	E. Loebe E. Jenner N. Austin P. Anspach
1952 — 33 T. H. Carruthers III	BB: BOS: WD: WB:	Ch. Meldon's Ruffian Ker-Mar Truly Fair of Abingdon Kenhoff's I'm It Ker-Mar Truly Fair of Abingdon	Payne Marquardt Snowden Marquardt
1951 — 18 R. R. Kerns, Jr.	BB: BOS: WD: WB:	Ch. Wilkern Fillip Nicomur Marsala Benrook Banning Nicomur Marsala	Feldman Daks MacMar Kls. Daks

Ch. Yankee Pride Colonel Stump (1956-1971). BOS, AMSCS, October 1958; BB, 1959, 1960, 1961 Westminster Shows; BB, 1959 and 1960 AMS CS, New York; BB, 1959 AMS CS, Pennsylvania; BB, 1962 International Kennel Club Show.

Ch. Cristy Lee's Frosty Jack (picture taken from Pasadena Kennel Club Dog Show in 1970). WD, 1970 Westminster; WD, 1970 AMS CS, New York; and BB, 1971 AMS CS, New York.

Year—Dogs in competition—Judge	Winners	Owners
1950 — 18 T. Keator	BB: Ch. Dorem Display BOS: Yankee Pride Vickie WD: Yankee Pride Cricket WB: Yankee Pride Vickie	Meldon Babisch Babisch Babisch
1949 — 13 E. Danks	BB: Demetrius of Harmert BOS: Gracon's Penelope v. Kalenheim WD: Demetrius of Harmert WB: Gracon's Penelope v. Kalenheim	Steineke Heim Steineke Heim
1948 — 7 W. L. Kendrick	BB: Dorem Discovery BOS: Rani of Kenhoff WD: Dorem Discovery WB: Rani of Kenhoff	MacKinney Warner MacKinney Warner
1947 — 3 W. F. Meyer	BB: Dorem Dynaree BOS: Meldon's Blackout WD: Meldon's Blackout WB: Dorem Dynaree	Daks Bruknis Bruknis Daks
1946 — 3 A. Rosenberg	BB: Dorem High Test BOS: Karen of Marienhof WD: Butler of Marienhof WB: Karen of Marienhof	Meldeon Rooks Bauhof Rooks

Ch. Blythewood Ricochet of LaMay